Classic
LOVE STORIES

Classic
LOVE STORIES

Sixteen Timeless Tales of Romance

EDITED AND WITH
AN INTRODUCTION *by*
LISA PURCELL

THE LYONS PRESS
GUILFORD, CONNECTICUT
AN IMPRINT OF THE GLOBE PEQUOT PRESS

Special contents of this edition copyright © 2005
by The Lyons Press

The Lyons Press is an imprint of The Globe Pequot Press.

Printed in the United States of America

10   9   8   7   6   5   4   3   2   1

Book design by Claire Zoghb

ISBN 1-59228-286-5

Library of Congress Cataloging-in-Publication Data
is available on file.

To the one who wrote in sugar on a tabletop
and to Laura and Drew Snodgrass,
a real-life classic love story.

Contents

CONTENTS

Introduction

So far only one incontestable truth has been uttered about love: "This is a great mystery."

—Anton Chekhov

L ove may be a mystery, but it has been a constant throughout the ages. From the first recorded history to the present day, historians, playwrights, writers, and poets have attempted to chronicle it, immortalize it, or simply celebrate it.

While love may be a constant, how love stories are told does change. In the past, emotions were no less strongly or deeply felt, but literary expression was far less explicit. The stories in this collection, written from the early 1800s to the early 1900s, are often far more subtle than contemporary romantic fiction.

None of them feature a "sex scene" and less than half of them have clear-cut happy endings. Yet, each in its own way offers us a clue to the mystery of love.

Russian writer Anton Chekhov avoids any easy generalizations about the essence of love. "It's best to interpret each instance separately in my view, without trying to generalize. We must isolate each individual case," decides Alehin in "About Love." While hosting two friends who have been caught in a storm, Alehin's talk turns to love—and its meaning. He tells his friends the story of Anna Alexyevna, his one great love. His is a story of missed chances; he lets his worries over the practical aspects of life and the opinions of others keep him from declaring himself to Anna until she has boarded the train that will take her from his life forever. Alehin will never know what might have been if he had acted sooner.

English writer Charlotte Mew, who Virginia Woolf called the "greatest living poetess," offers us a character who is surely Alehin's opposite in "Some Ways of Love." Smitten with an older woman, Captain Henley does not hesitate to propose to her. But Lady Hopedene sees only an impetuous boy before her and cruelly—or kindly—sends him away for a year. "If you do come back to me . . . I promise to treat you like a man," she says. Her test to ensure his constancy provides each of them a lesson in the many ways of love.

There may be many ways of love, but many people believe that there may be only one true love for each of us. But how do we know when we have found the right person?

Best known for his translation of Goethe's *Faust* and his poetry, Bayard Taylor turns to the short story genre to explore the nature of attraction in "Who Was She?" While on holiday, a young man finds a sketchbook in a hidden dell. Scattered throughout its pages are tantalizing snippets of writing—obviously penned in a woman's hand. "The men I seek *must* exist; where are they?" she wonders. Intrigued, he vows to find the sketchbook's owner. Will he also find his soul mate? Unearthing her identity, however, proves to be far more difficult that he anticipated. Even after he receives a reply to his newspaper advertisement, the enigmatic woman does not reveal herself—she is convinced that some "mysterious magnetic force" should bring them together.

Sherwood Anderson, author of the acclaimed *Winesburg, Ohio,* continues the theme of mysterious forces that attract one person to another in "The Other Woman." A man, whose life seems to be perfect, finds himself (on the eve of his marriage to a young woman he professes to love) attracted to the wife of the local tobacconist. Not only is she older than him, in his opinion, she is also "a very ordinary person with nothing special or notable about her."

Yet, he becomes obsessed with his desire for her. But can his desire for another woman coexist with the genuine love he feels for his bride?

Known for her stories that questioned the social mores and standards of late-nineteenth-century America, Kate Chopin, in "The Kiss," features a spoiled young protagonist who is well aware that love and marriage clearly do not *always* go together. She has set her sights on Brantain, who is neither handsome nor dynamic, but *is* very wealthy. A kiss from an "intimate friend of long standing" almost spoils her plan to catch her rich suitor *and* spoils her plan for her friend, too.

The narrator of French writer Emile Zola's story has a plan, too. He sits his companion, Nanon, down by the fireside to amuse her on a dreary, wet December night with the tale of "The Fairy Amoureuse," who emerges from an elusive flower, "seeking lonely hearts and bringing together those who sigh in solitude." She successfully unites the hero and heroine of the story, and also helps further the suit of the besotted storyteller. Updating another classic fairy tale, Louisa May Alcott writes a warm story of old friends, John and Nan, whose love for each other stands the trial of separation in "A Modern Cinderella."

Reggie, the hero in "Mr. and Mrs. Dove" by master short-story writer Katherine Mansfield, will soon be leaving England but, unlike Alcott's John, is unwilling to let time decide whether he belongs with the woman he loves. Rich, popular Anne, although she has warm feelings for Reggie, decides she just cannot marry him. For some reason, she always has an overwhelming urge to laugh when he is with her—she simply can't help it. But a pair of doves may show her a lesson in what makes a relationship really work.

English author, Ada Cambridge's "A Sweet Day" takes us from the birds to the bees—and to the Australian bush country, where she spent her life after marrying an Anglican minister. Lord Thomas de Bohan (or "Mr. Bone" as the egalitarian Aussies insist on calling him) leaves England hoping to experience some "real life." Weary of the glitter of the world's capitals, the Australian bush and its down-to-earth denizens are a welcome haven to him. It is here he meets Letty, a no-nonsense beekeeper, who is more interested in working with her hives than in flirting with an English nobleman.

A rural setting also frames "Love in a Garden," a light-hearted look at courtship from Henry Clay Lewis. First published under the pseudonym of "Madison Tensas," this story comes from a collection of tales from the "swamp doctor"—believed to be based on Lewis's own experience as a doctor in the remote Louisiana bayous. Big brawny Jerry finally finds something he fears when he decides that he wants to marry Mary. Will the grape arbor setting he chooses for the proposal prove romantic or stomach-churning?

"What She Wore" by Pulitzer Prize–winning Edna Ferber is also a humorous look at courtship, but is nonetheless touching. Here we meet Sophy Epstein, a wisecracking New Yorker who sells shoes in a downtown loft and wears a dress that is a bit too snug and has a V in the front cut a shade too low for propriety. Enter Louie, fresh from Oskaloosa, Iowa. Louie finds Sophy scandalous and she thinks he's a bit of a hayseed. But when he gets a new job and is about to leave the shoe store, she makes one or two minor adjustments to her simple black dress.

Love stories have been set in many places from mundane shoe stores to enchanted forests—and even telegraph offices. Walter P. Phillips was a journalist (eventually general manager of the Associated Press) and was also keenly interested in telegraphy (he even invented the "Phillips Code," a system using more than four thousand abbreviations and combinations of words that enabled telegraph companies to almost double the capacity of their wires). He was also known as the writer of many telegraph tales under the pen name of "John Oakum." In "Love and Lightning" he proves that long-distance love affairs could be successful even before the advent of telephones, e-mail, or frequent-flyer miles.

The next selection takes us from nineteenth-century America to Cromwell's England with a story by English writer Agnes Strickland. With a plot that could inspire a contemporary romance novel, "The Love Quarrel" introduces us to Helen Milbourne, the daughter of wealthy *parvenus,* who is in love with her neighbor, Colonel Dagworth, the son of an old and established family. Although a short story, "The Love Quarrel" packs abductions, rescues, betrayal, family feuds, political strife, and a happy ending into its quick-turning pages.

But even the truest of loves do not always get happy endings. Frederic Jesup Stimson, a Harvard-educated lawyer who wrote both novels and legal tomes, offers us "Mrs. Knollys," a poignant tale of a young English couple who honeymoons in the Alps. When tragedy strikes, the young bride proves that true love is timeless.

What collection calling itself *Classic Love Stories* could neglect the most famous love story of Western literature? This version of William Shakespeare's immortal tragedy *Romeo and Juliet* comes from Charles and Mary Lamb, who interwove their own writing with that of Shakespeare's to produce prose versions of twenty of his plays.

The collection closes with another classic, Frank Stockton's "The Lady, or the Tiger?" Set in the "very olden time," the beautiful daughter of a barbaric king falls in love with a courtier of low station. For his audacity, the young man is sentenced to face a cruel test in the public arena. There, he must choose between two doors: one holds a beautiful young woman who he will then marry; the other a fearsome and ravenous tiger. Before the day of the test, the princess finds out which door will lead to the lady and which to the tiger. When the fateful day arrives, she makes a subtle gesture to her lover. Which way did she direct him? Which will be more painful for her: watching his bloody, brutal death at the jaws of a tiger, or watching him fall into the welcoming arms of her lovely rival?

Classic
LOVE STORIES

About Love

[ANTON CHEKHOV]

At lunch next day there were very nice pies, crayfish, and mutton cutlets; and while we were eating, Nikanor, the cook, came up to ask what the visitors would like for dinner. He was a man of medium height, with a puffy face and little eyes; he was close-shaven, and it looked as though his moustaches had not been shaved, but had been pulled out by the roots. Alehin told us that the beautiful Pelagea was in love with this cook. As he drank and was of a violent character, she did not want to marry him, but was willing to live with him without. He was very devout, and his religious convictions would not allow him to "live in sin"; he insisted on her marrying him, and would consent to nothing else, and when he was drunk he used to abuse her and even beat her. Whenever he got drunk she used to hide upstairs and sob, and on such occasions Alehin and the servants stayed in the house to be ready to defend her in case of necessity.

We began talking about love.

"How love is born," said Alehin, "why Pelagea does not love somebody more like herself in her spiritual and external qualities, and why she fell in love with Nikanor, that ugly snout—we all call him 'The Snout'—how far questions of personal happiness are of consequence in love—all that is known; one can take what view one likes of it. So far only one incontestable truth has been uttered about love: 'This is a great mystery.' Everything else that has been written or said about love is not a conclusion, but only a statement of questions which have remained unanswered. The explanation which would seem to fit one case does not apply in a dozen others, and the very best thing, to my mind, would be to explain every case individually without attempting to generalize. We ought, as the doctors say, to individualize each case."

"Perfectly true," Burkin assented.

"We Russians of the educated class have a partiality for these questions that remain unanswered. Love is usually poeticized, decorated with roses, nightingales; we Russians decorate our loves with these momentous questions, and select the most uninteresting of them, too. In Moscow, when I was a student, I had a friend who shared my life, a charming lady, and every time I took her in my arms she was thinking what I would allow her a month for housekeeping and what was the price of beef a pound. In the same way, when we are in love we are never tired of asking ourselves questions: whether it is honorable or dishonorable, sensible or stupid, what this love is leading up to, and so on. Whether it is a good thing or not I don't know, but that it is in the way, unsatisfactory, and irritating, I do know."

It looked as though he wanted to tell some story. People who lead a solitary existence always have something in their hearts which they are eager to talk about. In town bachelors visit the baths and the restaurants on purpose to talk, and sometimes tell the most interesting things to bath attendants and waiters; in the country, as a rule, they unbosom themselves to their guests. Now from the window we could see a gray sky, trees drenched in the rain; in such weather we could go nowhere, and there was nothing for us to do but to tell stories and to listen.

"I have lived at Sofino and been farming for a long time," Alehin began, "ever since I left the University. I am an idle gentleman by education, a studious person by disposition; but there was a big debt owing on the estate when I came here, and as my father was in debt partly because he had spent so much on my education, I resolved not to go away, but to work till

I paid off the debt. I made up my mind to this and set to work, not, I must confess, without some repugnance. The land here does not yield much, and if one is not to farm at a loss one must employ serf labor or hired laborers, which is almost the same thing, or put it on a peasant footing—that is, work the fields oneself and with one's family. There is no middle path. But in those days, I did not go into such subtleties. I did not leave a clod of earth unturned; I gathered together all the peasants, men and women, from the neighboring villages; the work went on at a tremendous pace. I myself ploughed and sowed and reaped, and was bored doing it, and frowned with disgust, like a village cat driven by hunger to eat cucumbers in the kitchen-garden. My body ached, and I slept as I walked. At first it seemed to me that I could easily reconcile this life of toil with my cultured habits; to do so, I thought, all that is necessary is to maintain a certain external order in life. I established myself upstairs here in the best rooms, and ordered them to bring me there coffee and liquor after lunch and dinner, and when I went to bed, I read every night the *Yyesnik Evropi*. But one day our priest, Father Ivan, came and drank up all my liquor at one sitting; and the *Yyesnik Evropi* went to the priest's daughters; as in the summer, especially at the haymaking, I did not succeed in getting to my bed at all, and slept in the sledge in the barn, or somewhere in the forester's lodge, what chance was there of reading? Little by little I moved downstairs, began dining in the servants' kitchen, and of my former luxury nothing is left but the servants who were in my father's service, and whom it would be painful to turn away.

"In the first years I was elected here an honorary justice of the peace. I used to have to go to the town and take part in the sessions of the congress and of the circuit court, and this was a pleasant change for me. When you live here for two or three months without a break, especially in the winter, you begin at last to pine for a black coat. And in the circuit court there were frock coats, and uniforms, and dress-coats, too, all lawyers, men who have received a general education; I had someone to talk to. After sleeping in the sledge and dining in the kitchen, to sit in an armchair in clean linen, in thin boots, with a chain on one's waistcoat, is such luxury!

"I received a warm welcome in the town. I made friends eagerly. And of all my acquaintanceships, the most intimate and, to tell the truth, the most agreeable to me was my acquaintance with Luganovitch, the vice-president of the circuit court. You both know him: a most charming personality. It all happened just after a celebrated case of incendiarism; the preliminary investigation lasted two days; we were exhausted. Luganovitch looked at me and said:

" 'Look here, come round to dinner with me.'

"This was unexpected, as I knew Luganovitch very little, only officially, and I had never been to his house. I only just went to my hotel room to change and went off to dinner. And here it was my lot to meet Anna Alexyevna, Luganovitch's wife. At that time she was still very young, not more than twenty-two, and her first baby had been born just six months before. It is all a thing of the past; and now I should find it difficult to define what there was so exceptional in her, what it was in her attracted me so much; at the time, at dinner, it was all perfectly clear to me. I saw a lovely young, good, intelligent, fascinating woman, such as I had never met before; and I felt her at once some one close and already familiar, as though that face, those cordial, intelligent eyes, I had seen somewhere in my childhood, in the album which lay on my mother's chest of drawers.

"Four Jews were charged with being incendiaries, were regarded as a gang of robbers, and, to my mind, quite groundlessly. At dinner I was very much excited, I was uncomfortable, and I don't know what I said, but Anna Alexyevna kept shaking her head and saying to her husband:

" 'Dmitry, how is this?'

"Luganovitch is a good-natured man, one of those simple-hearted people who firmly maintain the opinion that once a man is charged before a court he is guilty, and to express doubt of the correctness of a sentence cannot be done except in legal form on paper, and not at dinner and in private conversation.

" 'You and I did not set fire to the place,' he said softly, 'and you see we are not condemned, and not in prison.'

"And both husband and wife tried to make me eat and drink as much as possible. From some trifling details, from the way they made the coffee together, for instance, and from the way they understood each other at half a word, I could gather that they lived in harmony and comfort, and that they were glad of a visitor. After dinner they played a duet on the piano; then it got dark, and I went home. That was at the beginning of spring.

"After that I spent the whole summer at Sofino without a break, and I had no time to think of the town, either, but the memory of the graceful fair-haired woman remained in my mind all those days; I did not think of her, but it was as though her light shadow were lying on my heart.

"In the late autumn there was a theatrical per-formance for some charitable object in the town. I went into the governor's box (I was invited to go there in the interval); I looked, and there was Anna Alexyevna sitting beside the governor's wife; and again the same irresistible, thrilling impression of beauty and sweet, caressing eyes, and again the same feeling of nearness. We sat side by side, then went to the foyer.

"'You've grown thinner,' she said; 'have you been ill?'

"'Yes, I've had rheumatism in my shoulder, and in rainy weather I can't sleep.'

"'You look dispirited. In the spring, when you came to dinner, you were younger, more confident. You were full of eagerness, and talked a great deal then; you were very interesting, and I really must confess I was a little carried away by you. For some reason you often came back to my memory during the summer, and when I was getting ready for the theatre today I thought I should see you.'

"And she laughed.

"'But you look dispirited today,' she repeated; 'it makes you seem older.'

"The next day I lunched at the Luganovitchs'. After lunch they drove out to their summer villa, in order to make arrangements there for the winter, and I went with them. I returned with them to the town, and at midnight drank tea with them in quiet domestic surroundings, while the fire glowed, and the young mother kept going to see if her baby girl was asleep. And after that, every time I went to town I never failed to visit the Luganovitchs. They grew used to me, and I grew used to them. As a rule I went in unannounced, as though I were one of the family.

"'Who is there?' I would hear from a faraway room, in the drawling voice that seemed to me so lovely.

"'It is Pavel Konstantinovitch,' answered the maid or the nurse.

"Anna Alexyevna would come out to me with an anxious face, and would ask every time:

"'Why is it so long since you have been? Has anything happened?'

"Her eyes, the elegant refined hand she gave me, her indoor dress, the way she did her hair, her voice, her step, always produced the same impression on me of something new and extraordinary in my life, and very important. We talked together for hours, were silent, thinking each our own thoughts, or she played for hours to me on the piano. If there were no one at home I stayed and waited, talked to the nurse, played with the child, or lay on the sofa in the study and read; and when Anna Alexyevna came back I met her in the hall, took all her parcels from her, and for some reason I carried those parcels every time with as much love, with as much solemnity, as a boy.

"There is a proverb that if a peasant woman has no troubles she will buy a pig. The Luganovitchs had no troubles, so they made friends with me. If I did not come to the town I must be ill or something must have happened to me, and both of them were extremely anxious. They were worried that I, an educated man with a knowledge of languages, should, instead of devoting myself to science or literary work, live in the country, rush round like a squirrel in a rage, work hard with never a penny to show for it. They fancied that I was unhappy, and that I only talked, laughed, and ate to conceal my sufferings, and even at cheerful moments when I felt happy I was aware of their searching eyes fixed upon me. They were particularly touching when I really was depressed, when I was being worried by some creditor or had not money enough to pay interest on the proper day. The two of them, husband and wife, would whisper together at the window; then he would come to me and say with a grave face:

"'If you really are in need of money at the moment, Pavel Konstantinovitch, my wife and I beg you not to hesitate to borrow from us.'

"And he would blush to his ears with emotion. And it would happen that, after whispering in the same way at the window, he would come up to me, with red ears, and say:

"'My wife and I earnestly beg you to accept this present.'

"And he would give me studs, a cigar-case, or a lamp, and I would send them game, butter, and flowers from the country. They both, by the way, had considerable means of their own. In early days I often borrowed money, and was not very particular about it—borrowed wherever I could—but nothing in the world would have induced me to borrow from the Luganovitchs. But why talk of it?

"I was unhappy. At home, in the fields, in the barn, I thought of her; I tried to understand the mystery of a beautiful, intelligent young woman's marrying some one so uninteresting, almost an old man (her husband was over forty), and having children by him; to understand the mystery of this uninteresting, good, simple-hearted man, who argued with such wearisome good sense, at balls and evening parties kept near the more solid people, looking listless and superfluous, with a submissive, uninterested expression, as though he had been brought there for sale, who yet believed in his right to be happy, to have children by her; and I kept trying to understand why she had met him first and not me, and why such a terrible mistake in our lives need have happened.

"And when I went to the town I saw every time from her eyes that she was expecting me, and she would confess to me herself that she had had a peculiar feeling all that day and had guessed that I should come. We talked a long time, and were silent, yet we did not confess our love to each other, but timidly and jealously concealed it. We were afraid of everything that might reveal our secret to ourselves. I loved her tenderly, deeply, but I reflected and kept asking myself what our love could lead to if we had not the strength to fight against it. It seemed to be incredible that my gentle, sad love could all at once coarsely break up the even tenor of the life of her husband, her children, and all the household in which I was so loved and trusted. Would it be honorable? She would go away with me, but where? Where could I take her? It would have been a different matter if I had had a beautiful, interesting life—if, for instance, I had been struggling for the emancipation of my country, or had been a celebrated man of science, an artist or a painter; but as it was it would mean taking her from one everyday humdrum life to another as humdrum or perhaps more so. And how long would our happiness last? What would happen to her in case I was ill, in case I died, or if we simply grew cold to one another?

"And she apparently reasoned in the same way. She thought of her husband, her children, and of her mother, who loved the husband like a son. If she abandoned herself to her feelings she would have to lie, or else to tell the truth, and in her position either would have been equally terrible and inconvenient. And she was tormented by the question whether her love would bring me happiness—would she not complicate my life, which, as it was, was hard enough and full of all sorts of trouble? She fancied she was not young enough for me, that she was not industrious nor energetic enough to begin a new life, and she often talked to her husband of the importance of my marrying a girl of intelligence and merit who would be a capable housewife and a help to me— and she would immediately add that it would be difficult to find such a girl in the whole town.

"Meanwhile the years were passing. Anna Alexyevna already had two children. When I arrived at the Luganovitchs' the servants smiled cordially, the children shouted that Uncle Pavel Konstantinovitch had come, and hung on my neck; every one was overjoyed. They did not understand what was passing in my soul, and thought that I, too, was happy. Every one looked on me as a noble being. And grown-ups and children alike felt that a noble being was walking about their rooms, and that gave a peculiar charm to their manner towards me, as though in my presence their life, too, was purer and more beautiful. Anna Alexyevna and I used to go to the theatre together, always walking there; we used to sit side by side in the stalls, our shoulders touching. I would take the opera-glass from her hands without a word, and feel at that minute that she was near me, that she was mine, that we could not live without each other; but by some strange misunderstanding, when we came out of the theatre we always said good-bye and parted as though we were strangers. Goodness knows what people were saying about us in the town already, but there was not a word of truth in it all!

"In the latter years Anna Alexyevna took to going away for frequent visits to her mother or to her sister; she began to suffer from low spirits, she began to recognize that her life was spoilt and unsatisfied, and at times she did not care to see her husband nor her children. She was already being treated for neurasthenia.

"We were silent and still silent, and in the presence of outsiders she displayed a strange irritation in regard to me; whatever I talked about, she disagreed with me, and if I had an argument she sided with my opponent. If I dropped anything, she would say coldly:

"'I congratulate you.'

"If I forgot to take the opera-glass when we were going to the theatre, she would say afterwards:

"'I knew you would forget it.'

"Luckily or unluckily, there is nothing in our lives that does not end sooner or later. The time of parting came, as Luganovitch was appointed president in one of the western provinces. They had to sell their furniture, their horses, their summer villa. When they drove out to the villa, and afterwards looked back as they were going away, to look for the last time at the garden, at the green roof, every one was sad, and I realized that I had to say goodbye not only to the villa. It was arranged that at the end of August we should see Anna Alexyevna off to the Crimea, where the doctors were sending her, and that a little later Luganovitch and the children would set off for the western province.

"We were a great crowd to see Anna Alexyevna off. When she had said good-bye to her husband and her children and there was only a minute left before the third bell, I ran into her compartment to put a basket, which she had almost forgotten, on the rack, and I had to say good-bye. When our eyes met in the compartment our spiritual fortitude deserted us both; I took her in my arms, she pressed her face to my breast, and tears flowed from her eyes. Kissing her face, her shoulders, her hands wet with tears—oh, how unhappy we were!—I confessed my love for her, and with a burning pain in my heart I realized how unnecessary, how petty, and how deceptive all that had hindered us from loving was. I understood that when you love you must either, in your reasonings about that love, start from what is highest, from what is more important than happiness or unhappiness, sin or virtue in their accepted meaning, or you must not reason at all.

"I kissed her for the last time, pressed her hand, and parted for ever. The train had already started. I went into the next compartment—it was empty— and until I reached the next station I sat there crying. Then I walked home to Sofino. . ."

While Alehin was telling his story, the rain left off and the sun came out. Burkin and Ivan Ivanovitch went out on the balcony, from which there was a beautiful view over the garden and the millpond, which was shining now in the sunshine like a mirror. They admired it, and at the same time they were sorry that this man with the kind, clever eyes, who had told them this story with such genuine feeling, should be rushing round and round this huge estate like a squirrel on a wheel instead of devoting himself to science or something else which would have made his life more pleasant; and they thought what a sorrowful face Anna Alexyevna must have had when he said good-bye to her in the railway-carriage and kissed her face and shoulders. Both of them had met her in the town, and Burkin knew her and thought her beautiful.

Some Ways of Love

[CHARLOTTE MEW]

Les âmes sont presque impénétrables
les unes aux autres, et c'est ce qui vous
montre le néant cruel de l'amour.
(Souls are almost impenetrable to
each other, and it is this which
demonstrates to you the cruel
nothingness of love.)

"And so you send me away unanswered?" said
the young man, rising reluctantly, taking his
gloves from the table and glancing meanwhile at the obdurate little lady on the sofa, who
witnessed his distress with that quizzical kindness,
which distracted him, in her clear, rather humorous
blue eyes.

"I will give you an answer if you wish it."

"I would rather hope—you do give me a ray of hope?"

"Just a ray," she admitted, laughing, with the same disturbing air of indulgence. "But don't magnify it—one has a habit, I know, of magnifying 'rays'— and I don't want you to come back—if you do come back—with a whole blazing sun."

"You are very frank, and a little cruel."

"I am afraid I mean to be—both. It is so much better for you." She was twisting the rings round her small fingers while she spoke, as if the interview were becoming slightly wearisome.

"You treat me like a boy," he broke out, with youthful bitterness.

"Ah! the cruelest treatment one can give to boys," she answered, looking up at him with her hovering brilliant, vexatious smile. But meeting his clouded glance she paused, and abandoned temporarily the lighter line of argument.

"Forgive me, Captain Henley—"

He scanned the treacherous face to see if the appellation so sedately uttered were not designedly malicious, but her next words reassured him.

"I will be more serious. See—frankly, cruelly perhaps—I do not know my heart." She did not falter over the studied phrase. "You are not the first," observing his troubled features ruefully, as she dealt the innocent blow. "You may not be—the last."

It left her lips a little laboredly, despite its apparent levity, but he was too much absorbed to notice fine shades of accent, and she went on—"I am not so charming as you think me, but that's a foregone conclusion. Shall I say, not so charming as I seem? At eighteen I made—I will not suggest I was led into—a loveless marriage. It was a failure, of course. I do not want to make another. I shrink from help-ing, shall we say, you? to a similar mistake. You must pardon me if I admit I do look upon you as—young; for years, you know, are deceptive things—even with women."

His boyish face expressed annoyance.

"Ah! I meant you to smile, and you are frowning. I should not be outraged if any one offered me the indignity you resent so foolishly; but then I am not—fortunately or unfortunately—so young as you. Come, be reasonable," she urged, with a singular sweetness of persuasion: "if I do not know my mind, is it so strange in me to suppose that yours may change? Again forgive me if I anticipate you. I have been glib enough with 'nevers' and 'forevers' in my day; but I shun them. I listen to them with more caution now. 'Never,' 'forever,'" she repeated, and mused for a moment over the words. "I sometimes imagine one is only safe in speaking them on the threshold of another life than this. It is a fancy of mine we should not use them now. Please humor it."

"I am not so diffident, doubtful, nor possibly so cynical," he began; but she interposed with the wave of a little glittering hand.

"Precisely; therefore I warn you. Why," she proceeded, with an unmistakable note of tenderness, which he did not catch, "you are even younger than I thought. I am glad—heartily—that you are going to the front. Cut up as many rascals as you can—a little fighting will bring you a lot of wisdom, and—oh yes! I know what a brute I am!—you want it badly. Come back in a year with your V.C. or without it: anyhow, with an ounce or two of experience in your pocket, and, if you do come back to me"—he winced at the repetition of the "if" and the doubt implied by it—"I promise to treat you like a man."

"And give me my answer?"

"Yes." She pronounced it with sudden softness.

"Meanwhile?"

"Meanwhile, husband the 'ray' if you like, but don't extend it; and remember it pledges us both to nothing. You"—she rapidly substituted "we—are free."

"You are free of course, Lady Hopedene," he agreed, with becoming solemnity. "I shall always consider myself bound. I—I—should like you to know that I do not consider myself free."

"As it please you," she yielded, with a flash of amusement shot at the melancholy countenance.

"It will be my only consolation," he returned, with ponderous sadness.

"So be it, then: I mustn't rob you of that. But remember, if the occasion calls, that I acquit you absolutely from reappearance at this bar."

A slight break in her voice reminded her that the time had come for his dismissal, and she proceeded promptly: "Now we must say Good-bye."

"Only *au revoir*."

"You are very literal; I like the old phrase best." She rose and took his hand, holding it longer than usual; and he looked down at her perturbedly. "Am I to have only a frown to keep?"

"Keep that," he cried, suddenly stooping to kiss the frail white fingers in his palm.

Then he turned away quickly, went out, and closed the door, missing, behind it, that curious fragrance of her presence, fresh and keen like morning air in meadows, subtler and sweeter than the faint perfume that hung about her person.

She stood motionless, tasting his departure: the smile which she had given him leave to take had faded from her eyes, and they were staring blankly at the door.

"Have I done well—for him?" she asked herself. "He may—he will—surely meet other women perhaps less scrupulous than I. And for myself?" She went towards a mirror set between the windows, and studied critically the reflection that faced her there. It showed a diminutive, delicately tinted face, beneath the childishly fair hair waved carefully above it, and for the moment, robbed of its insouciance, it looked wistful and a little wan. "I can spare a year," she decided, after a pause of close regard, "and at any rate my conscience is delightfully clear. My heart—'I do not know my heart.'" She laughed unsteadily. "He swallowed that absurdity; he might have read—bah," she cried, throwing her hands out with a gesture caught abroad, sometimes recurring with other un-English tricks of manner. "He is too young to read anything without a stammer yet. A woman has no right to take advantage of such a boy's first fancy. Assuredly I have done well."

She went back to the sofa and rested her head among the vivid cushions. When at length she raised it, the gay blue eyes were dim.

II

The *Nubia* was homeward bound, and her passengers were experiencing the inconveniences incidental to a passage through the Red Sea. Now and then the picturesque figure of a lascar darted across the semi-darkness. The stewards were throwing the mattresses upon the deck under a starlit sky. The captain and his first office had just surprised a *tête-à-tête* taking place in a quiet corner of the ship, with diversified feelings of annoyance.

"Is Henley serious?" the former inquired irritably. "Because it's a deuced awkward business. Miss Playfair is in my charge, and it isn't the first time I have had trouble over little affairs of the kind. Relatives are always unreasonable—even other people's relatives—but, by Jove, I think the attractive objects of their solicitude are worse."

"They met in India, so I suppose it's all right," returned the young man curtly, disinclined to discuss a situation which inspired him personally with a sensation of despair.

"I shall be glad to see Plymouth and the last of such an embarrassing cargo," returned the captain, turning on his heel.

"*Moi aussi*," muttered the young lieutenant sulkily.

But the subjects of this brief discourse did not apparently share these sentiments of relief at the prospect of gaining port.

"In spite of this awful heat, I wish it would never end," a deep voice proclaimed from the darkness. "It's ideal! The sea and the sky, this glorious sense of solitude, and you and I the only people on earth, it seems, in the midst of it. Say"—in a lower key—"you wish it might never end."

"What is the good of wishing, when you persist that it must end when we go ashore?"

"The gods may be merciful."

"You mean Lady Hopedene may be—cold?"

"She is always cold; a lovely little piece of ice. She never cared a hang for me, Mildred, or don't you think she must have betrayed it then?"

"I suppose she wanted to see what stuff you were made of. Why did she give you the chance of going back?"

"It was only a manner (she has a charming manner) of saying 'No.' Women"—he pronounced it with an air of profundity—"don't try experiments on the men they love."

"Then why go back at all? It is only inviting humiliation, if that's your view of it." Her tone, usually languorous, took a brisker note.

"I must, dearest: I gave my word."

"But you say she insisted upon not pledging you?"

"I pledged myself."

"You are too quixotic. Suppose you find her consoled?"

"Let us suppose it,"—he seized her hands—"the other possibility stuns me, let us forget it. Tonight, tomorrow, and still tomorrow are ours. Mildred—"

She released herself. "How can we forget it? It poisons today, it blunts tomorrow. It makes a farce of—of everything."

"I ought not to have spoken," he said remorsefully, "and, but for that other fellow, I should have waited till I was free. Do you forgive me?"

"I do not know."

"Whatever happens, the world will never hold any woman for me but you."

"You have possibly said that before?"

"I was a young fool—she told me so; and, good heavens! I know it now."

"Tell me," she said, "let us walk about. What is this other woman like?"

"Let us forget her," he pleaded.

"I want to know."

"Very small and fair; remarkably fair and witty and—well, I hardly know how to put it, courageous: it was the kind of fine unfeminine courage she seemed to have, that—that trapped my fancy. It struck me as an uncommon trait; if she had been a man she would have been cut out for a soldier. You see it was not love, darling; it began with a sort of impersonal admiration, and that's what it has come back to now."

"She will marry you," the girl assented conclusively. "I think I understand her better than you."

"And you will hate my memory?"

"Yes, for a time; and then—then I suppose I shall marry someone else."

"If I were you, I would rather spend my life alone."

"It is not so easy for women to talk or think of loneliness; but I love you, Alan," she ended passionately.

They bade each other a troubled and subdued goodnight.

III

> . . .*tandis que, dans le lointain, le*
> *cloche de la paroisse—emplissait l'air*
> *de vibrations douces, protectrices, con-*
> *seillères de bon sommeil à ceux qui ont*
> *encore des lendemains—*
> (. . .while, in the distance, the
> parish bell—filled the air with
> soft, protective vibrations, coun-
> selors of a good sleep to those for
> whom tomorrow will still
> come—)

Lady Hopedene closed the book brusquely, with the little recurrent foreign gesture of impatience.

"I must avoid this man; he is deplorably enervating." The china clock on the opposite wall struck four, and, summoned by its chime, the rejected phrase returned, to be rapidly dismissed again. *Ceux qui ont encore des lendemains.*

She passed a hand across her eyes, and pushed back the brilliant cushions against which her head rested uneasily. They framed the gold hair superbly, but seemed to have chased the delicate flush, once sweetly permanent, from the childish face. It looked out now from them nearly colorless and a little drawn.

The door opened, and a mechanical voice announced, "Captain Henley."

She did not rise, and he advanced towards her.

"Alan!" The name escaped her, poignant, even piteous in the suddenness and intensity of its utterance. A long succession of days, of weeks—a weight of waiting—seemed to be visibly thrust before him, painted on the wing of that swift cry.

And something more: behind it lurked a note of anguish, faint, but clashing audibly against its joy.

Insensibly he recoiled before the unfamiliar greeting. It was unlike her, unlike anything he had heard before. But in a moment the blue eyes, so strangely lit, resumed their old expression of half-bantering welcome; and she beckoned him forward, with the well-known wave of a small commanding hand.

"Come here, you wonderful apparition; I want to assure my senses, test my sanity. Is it actually *you*?"

"Unmistakably. I have come for my answer," he began briefly, hurriedly: aware that she had given it, before his question, in that startling and involuntary utterance of his name.

"You speak as if you were presenting a bill," she responded, laughing, "and the demand sounds somewhat peremptory, when I have been wondering if I should ever have to meet it. Oh, there are long arrears, I know," she added, taking his hand as he stood beside her. "Sit here." She made a place for him, and looked frankly, earnestly, at his slightly matured face.

"Why," she said, drawing back in mock alarm, "it *is* a man I have to deal with!" And then, with a quick and winning sweetness, "shall I tell you a secret, Captain Henley? I am rather disappointed, for—for—as a fact I loved the boy."

"Then why did you play with him?" he broke out, hardly able to control his bitterness, and returning her close gaze intently. "Your whim"—he spoke the truth baldly, careless, for the moment, whether or not she caught his meaning—"your whim has cost me much an honest answer would have saved me."

"You have a right, knowing so little, to reproach me. I will tell you," she returned gently. "It was after all, I suppose, mere egotism, because I cared for you more than myself. Your happiness was, is, will always, so I fancy, be more to me than mine."

An impulse came to him to put the truth before her, to tell his story plainly. For this woman whom he had loved inspired him strongly still with trust. Her mind, he knew, was sounder than the minds of other women he had met, and he could not fail to trust the heart that shone so clearly, straightly, through the blue eyes regarding him. He might have yielded to that momentary impulse, had she not broken in too hastily upon his wavering thought.

"I chose the most effectual lie that I could frame that day—do you remember?—when I told you that you were not the first, you might not be the last. You *are* the first"—her glance fell suddenly upon the yellow volume which had slipped, at his entrance, from the sofa to the floor—"you will be certainly the last. Lying always disgusts me. I pray you forgive my first and only lie."

He offered no response, but rose and stood silently, awkwardly beside her, loth to return her honesty with artificial protestation, knowing that speech was required of him, painfully seeking words.

She laughed, remembering him sometimes dumb of old, and went on with a trace of hesitation in her tone.

"My openness surprises you; but look at this," and she spread out before him a denuded, shrunken hand.

"How bare it is!" he said, taking it quietly in his own. "Where are the old adornments? Why have you forsaken them?"

She replied ruefully, "They have forsaken me. Perhaps"—she pointed lightly to her cheeks—"you have remarked that other adornments have turned traitors too. Sooner or later I must tell you: why not now? My physicians"—she pronounced the words with a mock pomposity, and punctuated them with a slight grimace—"give me a year, or not so long perhaps, for the pomps and vanities of this delightfully wicked world. And so, you see, out of pure consideration, the pomps and vanities are withdrawing gradually in preparation for their final exit."

She relinquished the accent of raillery, and began hurriedly and anxiously to caress his detaining hand. He seized her wrists and bent an incredulous glance upon her.

"It is some wretched jest. I do not believe you serious."

"Just now I am as serious as I shall ever be."

"You do not mean. . ." He could not achieve the obvious question, and stood holding the small fingers closely—stammering—silenced.

"Yes, truly, I have got marching orders, with a respite. There is a year for speech, for folly, for wisdom—if it were not so dull—and a year, my dear, for love."

"My G—!" he cried. "You have stunned me, Ella. You are here; I can see and hear you; but I can't manage to understand. It is like a nightmare. It isn't *true*?"

She released and laid her hands upon his arm, and checking his outburst with the flicker of a smile, protested—"You do not meet the enemy like a soldier."

"I have not your nerve," he answered. "Surely," he ventured, "some other man will give you hope or time."

She shook her head, and quoted lightly—"'If we die today, if we die tomorrow, there is little to choose. No man may speak when once the Fates have spoken.'"

Her eyes were challenging his to courage. "You loved your life far more than most of us," he said, immediately wishing the words back.

"I adored—I adore it. You link me with the past tense too readily. We will have no future nor sub-junctive moods, only the present and imperative. *Je t'aime—aime-toi, par example.*"

"Ella," he cried, "for God's sake be serious. I don't know how long you have known what you have told me. Remember it is new to me."

"It is passably new to me." She flashed a swift rebuke towards him from the brave blue eyes. "Do you wish me to play the coward?"

"You could not," he asserted brokenly. "You are a good soldier spoiled."

"The finest, if the clumsiest, compliment you have ever paid me."

"It is not that," he said almost roughly. "You shame me heart and soul; I feel like a deserter."

"They are cut after another pattern," she observed, with sweet decision. "We were neither of us made to turn our backs upon what lies before us or pull long faces at a foe. Through this long year— I will confess to a weary year—it never occurred to me as a reality that you would fail. I thought you might—I did not fear you *would*; but if you had, I should have faced it, and it would have been harder to face than death."

"I will never fail you," he said determinately; and as the "never" left his lips, he recalled her little speech upon the employment of that far-reaching term; only safely to be spoken, she had said, as now he spoke it, upon the threshold of the grave. And then it flashed across him how that interview had been a curious prototype of this. Then they had touched on death and laughter, and looked forth, too, upon the passage of a year. This was the ending to that unreal dream. But he was not to view its empty structure; she should not spend last hours picking up the petals of his fallen love.

"I will not fail you," he repeated passionately.

She listened with some wonder to the reiterated phrase.

"My dear, I do not doubt you."

"I have not said what I came to say, Ella. Will you be my wife?"

He asked the question foreseeing its consequences, but impelled to it by something deeper and more grave than pity. For a moment, she did not reply. She had been standing by him, but now sat down and began to finger the embroidered cushion, while she framed her answer. It came at last, but slowly from so quick a speaker.

"Love," she said, "though we don't often think of it, has an extensive wardrobe. Everyone cannot wear his richest garment—we cannot, you and I. Let us be glad he offers us any, for without his charity we must indeed go bare. We can be comrades, you and I, and only that, I think. It is the sanest, the best compact possible, since lovers end as we may not. You will keep watch with me, as if we were both good friends, good soldiers, till the enemy strikes, and he *will* strike, you know."

"That is a cold night's watch," he forced himself to say, remembering her cry of greeting, and wondering how she kept such guard upon her heart.

"Warm enough," she said, "much warmer than the dawn which is to end it. You will wait and keep this watch with me?"

"I will do anything you bid me."

"Then I bid you cultivate a smile for all weathers, and not to shiver yet." She took his hand again and led him to the window, where the lamps were being lit beside the railings of the park. "It is spring outside; I noticed the trees in bud this morning. The Fates have not been too unkind. They have lent us all the seasons; summer, my favorite, is coming, and—you have come."

He stooped and caught and kissed the little fingers loosely clasping his.

"Your last kiss has found a friend," she whispered; "it has lain for a long while lonely there."

"Give me your rings," he suggested; "I will get them altered. I like to see you wearing them."

"Yes," she agreed, "it is stupid to give them up. I will send—no, I will fetch them myself, if you will excuse me."

Loosing his hand, she crossed the darkening room and left him there alone, confronting the first great problem of his life.

IV

Mildred Playfair rose and left her seat by the window to stand beside the fire. She was renewing, without much display of friendliness, her acquaintance with an English spring. Henley was standing by the mantelpiece, and her movement brought them face to face. She lifted her dark eyes to his, and remarked, with the lingering intonation habitual to her, "There seems to be nothing more to say; I almost wonder why you came."

"Because you sent for me. I have put everything before you—the case as it stands, as it must stand for me. Perhaps it was better to come and tell you myself."

"You need not have waited for my summons."

"I meant to write. I thought it would be less painful for us both. It wasn't an easy matter, though. I was making a bungling attempt at an explanation on paper when your letter came."

"The explanation that you were going to relinquish me for a poetic and almost feminine fancy?"

"I had no choice."

"I did not know that men went in for this kind of thing. I imagined they were more—definite."

"I did not know myself that I could have done it a month ago; but women—a good woman—can turn a man inside out sometimes, and show him what he can and cannot do."

She had been holding her hands towards the fire, but now she turned and took from a table an Indian paper-knife and began slipping it in and out the uncut pages of a magazine.

"The fact is that you love this other woman still."

He hesitated, experiencing an almost Puritan desire to speak the barest truth.

"Not in the way you mean. I have learned this week that there are many ways of love."

"Is that original?" she asked, running a finger up and down the carved blade in her hand. "Are you sure you are not echoing a phrase of hers?"

"Perhaps. Mildred," he cried, "you make things even harder than they were. If you saw my heart, you would know I am not a traitor—at least to you."

To that other, he did not feel that he was playing altogether an untreacherous part.

"Your intricacies elude me. I admit I do not understand your way—your 'ways.'"

"Not after I have told you everything: when I have begged you to wait for me, as perhaps I ought not, as I surely should not have done if I did not care for you so much, dread losing you so terribly?"

"You must have known I should not consent to see you implicitly the lover of another woman."

"I am not her lover," he said briefly.

"Another fine distinction which I cannot grasp."

"If you could see my heart—" he began again; but she broke in.

"I can see enough of it to know it is not wholly mine."

"Do you want protestations?" he asked heavily, but without bitterness. "How can I make them now, with your refusal—with the vanity of hope—before me, with nothing but good-bye to say?"

"If you cared, you would not say it!"

Again he repeated, "I have no choice."

"Because you have chosen."

"In my heart, in my soul, I have chosen you."

"And yet you are going back to someone else?"

"For a year, and possibly less than that. Cannot you look at it as I do? We have life before us, but there is death in her eyes—death already, as I saw it, upon her lips. There is the grave between us," he urged, and ended with a new note of sadness. "Isn't that space enough?"

"It is invisible," she returned, "so do not blame me if I cannot see it. I can see only that there is a woman, or her shadow, between you and me."

"Is that your last word?" he asked, almost at that moment hoping it might be, aware that words had availed them little—brought no illumination and no relief.

"No," she broke forth suddenly, doffing the coldness and the calmness of her attitude petulantly, like an overweighted garment. "My last word is that I love you, Alan, and that by your own admission you belong to me." She crossed the room and threw herself upon him—"I cannot and I will not let you go."

He caught her with a short, familiar cry of welcome, and held her for a second; then releasing her, he rested a hand upon her dark and slightly ruffled hair.

"So you will wait?"

He spoke simply his first thought; but at its utterance she sprang away.

"No, not that—not that."

"What, then?" he asked bewilderedly. "You will not trust me?"

"*She* trusted you," the girl exclaimed, letting through her lips, in this last moment of distraction, the reminder which had hovered behind them once or twice before. "*She* let you go; and though she does not know it, you have failed her, or so you say; indeed, I do not know what to believe of you."

"That is true," he said. "God knows that I have failed her; *that* is true."

"Give me a pledge that you will not fail *me*."

"What pledge?" he asked; and added passionately; "any, any I can give is yours."

"Give me the only credible one," she urged, "and stay with me."

He paused—perplexed, dubious, stung; swaying upon a second choice. To which woman did he owe most? They seemed, as he stood there irresolute, both stationed before his vision, calling upon him that he should not fail. The one more distant, miniature and frail, a form of fading loveliness, in the posture of halting life; the other—she who stood beside him—vigorous, beautiful, distinct and dear, her feet strongly planted upon the stair of youth. The physical contrast struck him forcibly, and yet it was not that which brought conclusion to his contending thought. It was a sentence, spoken sweetly by a decisive voice proceeding from a chamber, which to his view was dimmer than the room wherein he stood—"We were neither of us made to turn our backs upon what lies before us or pull long faces at a foe."

"You will not trust me?" he asked again, this time with a dull accent of humility that might not have missed an older heart.

"I cannot," she replied rebelliously.

He met the dark, unyielding eyes, to find they stated an unyielding fact.

The woman who compelled it could not hear his answer; she would have understood it.

"And I," he said simply, with a regret that reached beyond the passion of the moment, "I cannot stay."

Who Was She?

[BAYARD TAYLOR]

Come, now, there may as well be an end of this! Every time I meet your eyes squarely I detect the question just slipping out of them. If you had spoken it, or even boldly looked it; if you had shown in your motions the least sign of a fussy or fidgety concern on my account; if this were not the evening of my birthday, and you the only friend who remembered it; if confession were not good for the soul, though harder than sin to some people, of whom I am one—well, if all reasons were not at this instant converged into a focus, and burning me rather violently, in that region where the seat of emotion is supposed to lie, I should keep my trouble to myself.

Yes, I have fifty times had it on my mind to tell you the whole story. But who can be certain that his best friend will not smile—or, what is worse, cherish a kind of charitable pity ever afterward—when the external forms of a very serious kind of passion seem trivial, fantastic, foolish? And the worst of all is that the heroic part which I imagined I was playing proves to have been almost the reverse. The only comfort which I can find in my humiliation is that I am capable of feeling it. There isn't a bit of a paradox in this, as you will see; but I only mention it now to prepare you for, maybe, a little morbid sensitiveness of my moral nerves.

The documents are all in this portfolio under my elbow. I had just read them again completely through when you were announced. You may examine them as you like afterward: for the present, fill your glass, take another Cabaña, and keep silent until my "ghastly tale" has reached its most lamentable conclusion.

The beginning of it was at Wampsocket Springs three years ago last summer. I suppose most unmarried men who have reached, or passed, the age of thirty—and I was then thirty-three—experience a milder return of their adolescent warmth, a kind of fainter second spring, since the first has not fulfilled its promise. Of course I wasn't clearly conscious of this at the time: who is? But I had had my youthful passion and my tragic disappointment as you know: I had looked far enough into what Thackeray used to call the cryptic mysteries to save me from the

Scylla of dissipation and yet preserved enough of natural nature to keep me out of the Pharisaic Charybdis. My devotion to my legal studies had already brought me a mild distinction; the paternal legacy was a good nest egg for the incubation of wealth—in short, I was a fair, respectable "party," desirable to the humbler mammas, and not to be despised by the haughty exclusives.

The fashionable hotel at the Springs holds three hundred, and it was packed. I had meant to lounge there for a fortnight and then finish my holidays at Long Branch; but eighty, at least, out of the three hundred were young and moved lightly in muslin. With my years and experience I felt so safe that to walk, talk, or dance with them became simply a luxury such as I had never—at least so freely—possessed before. My name and standing, known to some families, were agreeably exaggerated to the others, and I enjoyed that supreme satisfaction which a man always feels when he discovers, or imagines, that he is popular in society. There is a kind of premonitory apology implied in my saying this, I am aware. You must remember that I am culprit and culprit's counsel at the same time.

You have never been at Wampsocket? Well, the hills sweep around in a crescent on the northern side, and four or five radiating glens descending from them unite just above the village. The central one, leading to a waterfall (called "Minne-hehe" by the irreverent young people because there is so little of it), is the fashionable drive and promenade; but the second ravine on the left, steep, crooked, and cumbered with boulders which have tumbled from somewhere and lodged in the most extraordinary groupings, became my favorite walk of a morning. There was a footpath in it, well trodden at first, but gradually fading out as it became more like a ladder than a path, and I soon discovered that no other city feet than mine were likely to scale a certain rough slope which seemed the end of the ravine. With the aid of the tough laurel-stems I climbed to the top, passed through a cleft as narrow as a doorway, and presently found myself in a little upper dell, as wild and sweet and strange as one of the pictures that haunts us on the brink of sleep.

There was a pond—no, rather a bowl—of water in the center; hardly twenty yards across, yet the sky in it was so pure and far down that the circle of rocks and summer foliage enclosing it seemed like a little planetary ring floating off alone through space. I can't explain the charm of the spot, nor the selfishness which instantly suggested that I should keep the discovery to myself. Ten years earlier I should have looked around for some fair spirit to be my "minister," but now—

One forenoon—I think it was the third or fourth time I had visited the place—I was startled to find the dent of a heel in the earth, halfway up the slope. There had been rain during the night and the earth was still moist and soft. It was the mark of a woman's boot, only to be distinguished from that of a walking stick by its semicircular form. A little higher, I found the outline of a foot, not so small as to awake an ecstasy, but with a suggestion of lightness, elasticity, and grace. If hands were thrust through holes in a board-fence, and nothing of the attached bodies seen, I can easily imagine that some would attract and others repel us: with footprints the impression is weaker, of course, but we cannot escape it. I am not sure whether I wanted to find the unknown wearer of the boot within my precious personal solitude: I was afraid I should see her while passing through the rocky crevice, and yet was disappointed when I found no one.

But on the flat, warm rock overhanging the tarn— my special throne—lay some withering wildflowers and a book! I looked up and down, right and left: there was not the slightest sign of another human life than mine. Then I lay down for a quarter of an hour, and listened: there were only the noises of bird and squirrel, as before. At last, I took up the book, the flat breadth of which suggested only sketches. There were, indeed, some tolerable studies of rocks and trees on the first pages; a few not very striking caricatures, which seemed to have been commenced as portraits,

but recalled no faces I knew; then a number of frag-
mentary notes, written in pencil. I found no name,
from first to last; only, under the sketches, a monogram
so complicated and laborious that the initials could
hardly be discovered unless one already knew them.

The writing was a woman's, but it had surely
taken its character from certain features of her own:
it was clear, firm, individual. It had nothing of that
air of general debility which usually marks the manuscript of young ladies, yet its firmness was far
removed from the stiff, conventional slope which all
Englishwomen seem to acquire in youth and retain
through life. I don't see how any man in my situation could have helped reading a few lines—if only
for the sake of restoring lost property. But I was
drawn on, and on, and finished by reading all:
thence, since no further harm could be done, I reread,
pondering over certain passages until they stayed
with me. Here they are, as I set them down, that
evening, on the back of a legal blank:

"It makes a great deal of difference whether we
wear social forms as bracelets or handcuffs."

"Can we not still be wholly our independent
selves, even while doing, in the main, as others do? I
know two who are so; but they are married."

"The men who admire these bold, dashing young
girls treat them like weaker copies of themselves.
And yet they boast of what they call 'experience'!"

"I wonder if any one felt the exquisite beauty of the noon as I did today? A faint appreciation of sunsets and storms is taught us in youth, and kept alive by novels and flirtations; but the broad, imperial splendor of this summer noon!—and myself standing alone in it—yes, utterly alone!"

"The men I seek *must* exist: where are they? How make an acquaintance, when one obsequiously bows himself away, as I advance? The fault is surely not all on my side."

There was much more, intimate enough to inspire me with a keen interest in the writer, yet not sufficiently so to make my perusal a painful indiscretion. I yielded to the impulse of the moment, took out my pencil, and wrote a dozen lines on one of the blank pages. They ran something in this wise: "*Ignotus Ignotæ!*—You have bestowed without intending it, and I have taken without your knowledge. Do not regret the accident which has enriched another. This concealed idyl of the hills was mine, as I supposed, but I acknowledge your equal right to it. Shall we share the possession, or will you banish me?"

There was a frank advance, tempered by a proper caution, I fancied, in the words I wrote. It was evident that she was unmarried, but outside of that certainty there lay a vast range of possibilities, some of them alarming enough. However, if any nearer acquaintance should arise out of the incident, the next step must be taken by her. Was I one of the men she sought? I almost imagined so—certainly hoped so.

I laid the book on the rock, as I had found it, bestowed another keen scrutiny on the lonely land-scape, and then descended the ravine. That evening, I went early to the ladies' parlor, chatted more than usual with the various damsels whom I knew, and watched with a new interest those whom I knew not. My mind, involuntarily, had already created a picture of the unknown. She might be twenty-five, I thought; a reflective habit of mind would hardly be developed before that age. Tall and stately, of course; distinctly proud in her bearing, and somewhat reserved in her manners. Why she should have large dark eyes, with long dark lashes, I could not tell; but so I seemed to see her. Quite forgetting that I was (or had meant to be) *Ignotus*, I found myself staring rather significantly at one or the other of the young ladies, in whom I discovered some slight general resemblance to the imaginary character. My fancies, I must confess, played strange pranks with me. They had been kept in a coop so many years that now, when I suddenly turned them loose, their rickety attempts at flight quite bewildered me.

No! there was no use in expecting a sudden dis-covery. I went to the glen betimes, next morning:

the book was gone and so were the faded flowers, but some of the latter were scattered over the top of another rock, a few yards from mine. Ha! this means that I am not to withdraw, I said to myself: she makes room for me!

But how to surprise her?—for by this time I was fully resolved to make her acquaintance, even though she might turn out to be forty, scraggy, and sandy-haired.

I knew no other way so likely as that of visiting the glen at all times of the day. I even went so far as to write a line of greeting, with a regret that our visits had not yet coincided, and laid it under a stone on the top of *her* rock. The note disappeared, but there was no answer in its place. Then I suddenly remembered her fondness for the noon hours, at which time she was "utterly alone." The hotel *table d'hôte* was at one o'clock: her family, doubtless, dined later, in their own rooms. Why, this gave me, at least, her place in society! The question of age, to be sure, remained unsettled; but all else was safe.

The next day I took a late and large breakfast, and sacrificed my dinner. Before noon the guests had all straggled back to the hotel from glen and grove and lane, so bright and hot was the sunshine. Indeed, I could hardly have supported the reverberation of heat from the sides of the ravine, but for a fixed belief that I should be successful. While crossing the narrow meadow upon which it opened, I caught a glimpse of something white among the thickets higher up. A moment later it had vanished, and I quickened my pace, feeling the beginning of an absurd nervous excitement in my limbs. At the next turn, there it was again! but only for another moment. I paused, exulting, and wiped my drenched forehead. "She cannot escape me!" I murmured between the deep draughts of cooler air I inhaled in the shadow of a rock.

A few hundred steps more brought me to the foot of the steep ascent, where I had counted on overtaking her. I was too late for that, but the dry, baked soil had surely been crumbled and dislodged, here and there, by a rapid foot. I followed, in reckless haste, snatching at the laurel branches right and left, and paying little heed to my footing. About one-third of the way up I slipped, fell, caught a bush which snapped at the root, slid, whirled over, and before I fairly knew what had happened, I was lying doubled up at the bottom of the slope.

I rose, made two steps forward, and then sat down with a groan of pain; my left ankle was badly sprained, in addition to various minor scratches and bruises. There was a revulsion of feeling, of course— instant, complete, and hideous. I fairly hated the

Unknown. "Fool that I was!" I exclaimed, in the theatrical manner, dashing the palm of my hand softly against my brow: "lured to this by the fair traitoress! But no!—not fair: she shows the artfulness of faded, desperate spinsterhood; she is all compact of enamel, 'liquid bloom of youth' and hair dye!"

There was a fierce comfort in this thought, but it couldn't help me out of the scrape. I dared not sit still, lest a sunstroke should be added, and there was no resource but to hop or crawl down the rugged path, in the hope of finding a forked sapling from which I could extemporize a crutch. With endless pain and trouble I reached a thicket, and was feebly working on a branch with my penknife, when the sound of a heavy footstep surprised me.

A brown harvest-hand, in straw hat and shirt-sleeves, presently appeared. He grinned when he saw me, and the thick snub of his nose would have seemed like a sneer at any other time.

"Are you the gentleman that got hurt?" he asked. "Is it pretty tolerable bad?"

"Who said I was hurt?" I cried in astonishment.

"One of your town-women from the hotel—I reckon she was. I was binding oats, in the field over the ridge; but I haven't lost no time in comin' here."

While I was stupidly staring at this announcement, he whipped out a big clasp-knife, and in a few minutes fashioned me a practicable crutch. Then, taking me by the other arm, he set me in motion toward the village.

Grateful as I was for the man's help, he aggravated me by his ignorance. When I asked if he knew the lady, he answered: "It's more'n likely *you* know her better." But where did she come from? Down from the hill, he guessed, but it might ha' been up the road. How did she look? was she old or young? what was the color of her eyes? of her hair? There, now, I was too much for him. When a woman kept one o' them speckled veils over her face, turned her head away, and held her parasol between, how were you to know her from Adam? I declare to you, I couldn't arrive at one positive particular. Even when he affirmed that she was tall, he added, the next instant: "Now I come to think on it, she stepped mighty quick; so I guess she must ha' been short."

By the time we reached the hotel, I was in a state of fever; opiates and lotions had their will of me for the rest of the day. I was glad to escape the worry of questions, and the conventional sympathy expressed in inflections of the voice which are meant to soothe, and only exasperate. The next morning, as I lay upon my sofa, restful, patient, and properly cheerful, the waiter entered with a bouquet of wildflowers.

"Who sent them?" I asked.

"I found them outside your door, sir. Maybe there's a card; yes, here's a bit o' paper."

I opened the twisted slip he handed me, and read: "From your dell—and mine." I took the flowers; among them were two or three rare and beautiful varieties which I had only found in that one spot. Fool, again! I noiselessly kissed, while pretending to smell them, had them placed on a stand within reach, and fell into a state of quiet and agreeable contemplation.

Tell me yourself whether any male human being is ever too old for sentiment, provided that it strikes him at the right time and in the right way! What did that bunch of wildflowers betoken? Knowledge, first; then, sympathy; and finally, encouragement, at least. Of course she had seen my accident, from above; of course she had sent the harvest laborer to aid me home. It was quite natural she should imagine some special, romantic interest in the lonely dell, on my part, and the gift took additional value from her conjecture.

Four days afterwards, there was a hop in the large dining room of the hotel. Early in the morning, a fresh bouquet had been left at my door. I was tired of my enforced idleness, eager to discover the fair unknown (she was again fair, to my fancy!), and I determined to go down, believing that a cane and a crimson velvet slipper on the left foot would provoke a glance of sympathy from certain eyes, and thus enable me to detect them.

The fact was, the sympathy was much too general and effusive. Everybody, it seemed, came to me with kindly greetings; seats were vacated at my approach, even fat Mrs. Huxter insisting on my taking her warm place, at the head of the room. But Bob Leroy—you know him—as gallant a gentleman as ever lived, put me down at the right point, and kept me there. He only meant to divert me, yet gave me the only place where I could quietly inspect all the younger ladies, as dance or supper brought them near.

One of the dances was an old-fashioned cotillion, and one of the figures, the "coquette," brought every one, in turn, before me. I received a pleasant word or two from those whom I knew, and a long, kind, silent glance from Miss May Danvers. Where had been my eyes? She was tall, stately, twenty-five, had large dark eyes, and long dark lashes! Again the changes of the dance brought her near me; I threw (or strove to throw) unutterable meanings into my eyes, and cast them upon hers. She seemed startled, looked suddenly away, looked back to me, and— blushed. I knew her for what is called "a nice girl"—that is, tolerably frank, gently feminine, and not dangerously intelligent. Was it possible that I had overlooked so much character and intellect?

As the cotillion closed, she was again in my neighborhood, and her partner led her in my direction. I was rising painfully from my chair, when

Bob Leroy pushed me down again, whisked another seat from somewhere, planted it at my side, and there she was!

She knew who was her neighbor, I plainly saw; but instead of turning toward me, she began to fan herself in a nervous way and to fidget with the buttons of her gloves. I grew impatient.

"Miss Danvers!" I said at last.

"Oh!" was all her answer, as she looked at me for a moment.

"Where are your thoughts?" I asked.

Then she turned, with wide, astonished eyes, coloring softly up to the roots of her hair. My heart gave a sudden leap.

"How can you tell, if I cannot?" she asked.

"May I guess?"

She made a slight inclination of the head, saying nothing. I was then quite sure.

"The second ravine to the left of the main drive?"

This time she actually started; her color became deeper, and a leaf of the ivory fan snapped between her fingers.

"Let there be no more a secret!" I exclaimed. "Your flowers have brought me your messages; I knew I should find you—"

Full of certainty, I was speaking in a low, impassioned voice. She cut me short by rising from her seat; I felt that she was both angry and alarmed.

Fisher, of Philadelphia, jostling right and left in his haste, made his way toward her. She fairly snatched his arm, clung to it with a warmth I had never seen expressed in a ballroom, and began to whisper in his ear. It was not five minutes before he came to me, alone, with a very stern face, bent down, and said: "If you have discovered our secret, you will keep silent. You are certainly a gentleman."

I bowed, coldly and savagely. There was a draught from the open window; my ankle became suddenly weary and painful, and I went to bed. Can you believe that I didn't guess, immediately, what it all meant? In a vague way, I fancied that I had been premature in my attempt to drop our mutual incognito, and that Fisher, a rival lover, was jealous of me. This was rather flattering than otherwise; but when I limped down to the ladies' parlor, the next day no Miss Danvers was to be seen. I did not venture to ask for her; it might seem importunate, and a woman of so much hidden capacity was evidently not to be wooed in the ordinary way.

So another night passed by; and then, with the morning, came a letter which made me feel, at the same instant, like a fool and a hero. It had been dropped in the Wampsocket post office, was legibly addressed to me and delivered with some other letters which had arrived by the night mail. Here it is; listen!

"*Noto Ignota!*—Haste is not a gift of the gods, and you have been impatient, with the usual result. I was almost prepared for this, and thus am not wholly disappointed. In a day or two more you will discover your mistake, which, so far as I can learn, has done no particular harm. If you wish to find *me*, there is only one way to seek me; should I tell you what it is, I should run the risk of losing you—that is, I should preclude the manifestation of a certain quality which I hope to find in the man who may—or, rather, must—be my friend. This sounds enigmatical, yet you have read enough of my nature, as written in those random notes in my sketchbook, to guess, at least, how much I require. Only this let me add: mere guessing is useless.

"Being unknown, I can write freely, If you find me, I shall be justified; if not, I shall hardly need to blush, even to myself, over a futile experiment.

"It is possible for me to learn enough of your life, henceforth, to direct my relation toward you. This may be the end; if so, I shall know it soon. I shall also know whether you continue to seek me. Trusting in your honor as a man, I must ask you to trust in mine, as a woman."

I *did* discover my mistake, as the Unknown promised. There had been a secret betrothal between Fisher and Miss Danvers, and, singularly enough, the momentous question and answer had been given in the very ravine leading to my upper dell! The two meant to keep the matter to themselves; but therein, it seems, I thwarted them; there was a little opposition on the part of their respective families, but all was amicably settled before I left Wampsocket.

The letter made a very deep impression upon me. What was the one way to find her? What could it be but the triumph that follows ambitious toil—the manifestation of all my best qualities as a man? Be she old or young, plain or beautiful, I reflected, hers is surely a nature worth knowing, and its candid intelligence conceals no hazards for me. I have sought her rashly, blundered, betrayed that I set her lower, in my thoughts, than her actual self: let me now adopt the opposite course, seek her openly no longer, go back to my tasks, and, following my own aims vigorously and cheerfully, restore that respect which she seemed to be on the point of losing. For, consciously or not, she had communicated to me a doubt, implied in the very expression of her own strength and pride. She had meant to address me as an equal, yet, despite herself, took a stand a little above that which she accorded to me.

I came back to New York earlier than usual, worked steadily at my profession and with increasing success, and began to accept opportunities (which I had previously declined) of making myself personally known to the great, impressible, fickle, tyrannical public. One or two of my speeches in the hall of the Cooper Institute, on various occasions—as you may perhaps remember—gave me a good headway with the party, and were the chief cause of my nomination for the State office which I still hold. (There, on the table lies a resignation, written today, but not yet signed. We'll talk of it afterward.) Several months passed by, and no further letter reached me. I gave up much of my time to society, moved familiarly in more than one province of the kingdom here, and vastly extended my acquaintance, especially among the women; but not one of them betrayed the mysterious something or other—really I can't explain precisely what it was!—which I was looking for. In fact, the more I endeavored quietly to study the sex, the more confused I became.

At last I was subjected to the usual onslaught from the strong-minded.

A small but formidable committee entered my office one morning and demanded a categorical declaration of my principles. What my views on the subject were I knew very well; they were clear and decided; and yet I hesitated to declare them! It wasn't a temptation of Saint Anthony—that is, turned the other way—and the belligerent attitude of the dames did not alarm me in the least; but *she*! What was *her* position? How could I best please her? It flashed upon my mind, while Mrs.———— was making her formal speech, that I had taken no step for months without a vague, secret reference to *her*. So I strove to be courteous, friendly, and agreeably noncommittal; begged for further documents, and promised to reply by letter in a few days.

I was hardly surprised to find the well-known hand on the envelope of a letter shortly afterward. I held it for a minute in my palm, with an absurd hope that I might sympathetically feel its character before breaking the seal. Then I read it with a great sense of relief.

"I have never assumed to guide a man, except toward the full exercise of his powers. It is not opinion in action, but opinion in a state of idleness or indifference, which repels me. I am deeply glad that you have gained so much since you left the country. If, in shaping your course, you have thought of me, I will frankly say that *to that extent*, you have drawn nearer. Am I mistaken in conjecturing that you wish to know my relation to the movement concerning which you were recently interrogated? In this, as in other instances which may come, I must beg you to consider me only as a spectator. The more my own views may seem likely to sway your action, the less I shall be inclined to declare them. If you find this cold or unwomanly, remember that it is not easy!"

Yes! I felt that I had certainly drawn much nearer to her. And from this time on, her imaginary face and form became other than they were. She was twenty-eight—three years older; a very little above the middle height, but not tall; serene, rather than stately, in her movements; with a calm, almost grave face, relieved by the sweetness of the full, firm lips; and finally eyes of pure, limpid gray, such as we fancy belonged to the Venus of Milo. I found her thus much more attractive than with the dark eyes and lashes—but she did not make her appearance in the circles which I frequented.

Another year slipped away. As an official personage, my importance increased, but I was careful not to exaggerate it to myself. Many have wondered (perhaps you among the rest) at my success, seeing that I possess no remarkable abilities. If I have any secret, it is simply this—doing faithfully, with all my might, whatever I undertake. Nine-tenths of our politicians become inflated and careless, after the first few years, and are easily forgotten when they once lose place.

I am a little surprised now that I had so much patience with the Unknown. I was too important, at least, to be played with; too mature to be subjected to a longer test; too earnest, as I had proved, to be doubted, or thrown aside without a further explanation.

Growing tired, at last, of silent waiting, I bethought me of advertising. A carefully written "Personal," in which *Ignotus* informed *Ignota* of the necessity of his communicating with her, appeared simultaneously in the *Tribune, Herald, World*, and *Times*. I renewed the advertisement as the time expired without an answer, and I think it was about the end of the third week before one came, through the post, as before.

Ah, yes! I had forgotten. See! my advertisement is pasted on the note, as a heading or motto for the manuscript lines. I don't know why the printed slip should give me a particular feeling of humiliation as I look at it, but such is the fact. What she wrote is all I need read to you:

"I could not, at first, be certain that this was meant for me. If I were to explain to you why I have not written for so long a time, I might give you one of the few clues which I insist on keeping in my own hands. In your public capacity, you have been (so far as a woman may judge) upright, independent, wholly manly: in your relations with other men I learn nothing of you that is not honorable: toward women you are kind, chivalrous, no doubt, overflowing with the *usual* social refinements, but—Here, again, I run hard upon the absolute necessity of silence. The way to me, if you care to traverse it, is so simple, so very simple! Yet, after what I have written, I cannot even wave my hand in the direction of it, without certain self-contempt. When I feel free to tell you, we shall draw apart and remain unknown forever.

"You desire to write? I do not prohibit it. I have heretofore made no arrangement for hearing from you, in turn, because I could not discover that any advantage would accrue from it. But it seems only fair, I confess, and you dare not think me capricious. So, three days hence, at six o'clock in the evening, a trusty messenger of mine will call at your door. If you have anything to give her for me, the act of giving it must be the sign of a compact on your part that you will allow her to leave immediately, unquestioned and unfollowed."

You look puzzled, I see: you don't catch the real drift of her words? Well, that's a melancholy encouragement. Neither did I, at the time: it was plain that I had disappointed her in some way, and my intercourse with or manner toward women had something to do with it. In vain I ran over as much of my later social life as I could recall. There had been no special attention, nothing to mislead a susceptible heart; on the other side, certainly no rudeness, no want of "chivalrous" (she used the word!) respect and attention. What, in the name of all the gods, was the matter?

In spite of all my efforts to grow clearer, I was obliged to write my letter in a rather muddled state of mind. I had *so* much to say! Sixteen folio pages, I was sure, would only suffice for an introduction to the case; yet, when the creamy vellum lay before me and the moist pen drew my fingers towards it, I sat stock dumb for half an hour. I wrote, finally, in a half-desperate mood, without regard to coherency or logic. Here's a rough draft of a part of the letter, and a single passage from it will be enough:

"I can conceive of no simpler way to you than the knowledge of your name and address. I have drawn airy images of you, but they do not become incarnate, and I am not sure that I should recognize you in the brief moment of passing. Your nature is not of those which are instantly legible. As an abstract power, it has wrought in my life and it continually moves my heart with desires which are unsatisfactory because so vague and ignorant. Let me offer you, personally, my gratitude, my earnest friendship: you would laugh if I were *now* to offer more."

Stay! here is another fragment, more reckless in tone:

"I want to find the woman whom I can love— who can love me. But this is a masquerade where the features are hidden, the voice disguised, even the hands grotesquely gloved. Come! I will venture more than I ever thought it was possible to me. You shall know my deepest nature as I myself seem to know it. Then, give me the commonest chance of learning yours, through an intercourse which shall leave both free, should we not feel the closing of the inevitable bond!"

After I had written that, the pages filled rapidly. When the appointed hour arrived, a bulky epistle, in a strong linen envelope, sealed with five wax seals, was waiting on my table. Precisely at six there was an announcement: the door opened, and a little outside, in the shadow, I saw an old woman, in a threadbare dress of rusty black.

"Come in!" I said.

"The letter!" answered a husky voice. She stretched out a bony hand, without moving a step.

"It is for a lady—very important business," said I, taking up the letter; "are you sure that there is no mistake?"

She drew her hand under the shawl, turned without a word, and moved toward the hall door.

"Stop!" I cried: "I beg a thousand pardons! Take it—take it! You are the right messenger!"

She clutched it, and was instantly gone.

Several days passed, and I gradually became so nervous and uneasy that I was on the point of inserting another "Personal" in the daily papers, when the answer arrived. It was brief and mysterious; you shall hear the whole of it:

"I thank you. Your letter is a sacred confidence which I pray you never to regret. Your nature is sound and good. You ask no more than is reasonable, and I have no real right to refuse. In the one respect which I have hinted, I may have been unskillful or too narrowly cautious: I must have the certainty on this. Therefore, as a generous favor, give me six months more! At the end of that time I will write to you again. Have patience with these brief lines: another word might be a word too much."

You notice the change in her tone? The letter gave me the strongest impression of a new, warm, almost anxious interest on her part. My fancies, as first at Wampsocket, began to play all sorts of singular pranks: sometimes she was rich and of an old family, sometimes moderately poor and obscure, but always the same calm reposeful face and clear gray eyes. I ceased looking for her in society, quite sure that I should not find her, and nursed a wild expectation of suddenly meeting her, face to face, in the most unlikely places and under startling circumstances. However, the end of it all was patience—patience for six months.

There's not much more to tell; but this last letter is hard for me to read. It came punctually, to a day. I knew it would, and at the last I began to dread the time, as if a heavy note were falling due, and I had no funds to meet it. My head was in a whirl when I broke the seal. The fact in it stared at me blankly, at once, but it was a long time before the words and sentences became intelligible.

"The stipulated time has come, and our hidden romance is at an end. Had I taken this resolution a year ago, it would have saved me many vain hopes, and you, perhaps, a little uncertainty. Forgive me, first, if you can, and then hear the explanation:

"You wished for a personal interview: *you have had, not one, but many.* We have met, in society, talked face to face, discussed the weather, the opera, toilettes, Queechy, Aurora Floyd, Long Branch and Newport, and exchanged a weary amount of fashionable gossip; and you never guessed that I was governed by any deeper interest! I have purposely uttered ridiculous platitudes, and you were as smilingly courteous as if you enjoyed them: I have let fall remarks whose hollowness and selfishness could not have escaped you, and have waited in vain for a word of sharp, honest, manly reproof. Your manner to me was unexceptionable, as it was to all other women: but there lies the source of my disappointment, of— yes—of my sorrow!

"You appreciate, I cannot doubt, the qualities in woman which men value in one another—culture, independence of thought, a high and earnest apprehension of life; but you know not how to seek them.

It is not true that a mature and unperverted woman is flattered by receiving only the general obsequiousness which most men give to the whole sex. In the man who contradicts and strives with her, she discovers a truer interest, a nobler respect. The empty-headed, spindle-shanked youths who dance admirably, understand something of billiards, much less of horses, and still less of navigation, soon grow inexpressibly wearisome to us; but the men who adopt their social courtesy, never seeking to arouse, uplift, instruct us, are a bitter disappointment.

"What would have been the end, had you really found me? Certainly a sincere, satisfying friendship. No mysterious magnetic force has drawn you to me or held you near me, nor has my experiment inspired me with an interest which cannot be given up without a personal pang. I am grieved, for the sake of all men and all women. Yet, understand me! I mean no slightest reproach. I esteem and honor you for what you are. Farewell!"

There! Nothing could be kinder in tone, nothing more humiliating in substance. I was sore and offended for a few days; but I soon began to see, and ever more and more clearly, that she was wholly right. I was sure, also, that any further attempt to correspond with her would be in vain. It all comes of taking society just as we find it, and supposing that conventional courtesy is the only safe ground on which men and women can meet.

The fact is—there's no use in hiding it from myself (and I see, by your face, that the letter cuts into your own conscience)—she is a free, courageous, independent character, and—I am not.

But who *was* she?

The Other Woman

[SHERWOOD ANDERSON]

"I am in love with my wife," he said—a superfluous remark, as I had not questioned his attachment to the woman he had married. We walked for ten minutes and then he said it again. I turned to look at him. He began to talk and told me the tale I am now about to set down.

The thing he had on his mind happened during what must have been the most eventful week of his life. He was to be married on Friday afternoon. On Friday of the week before he got a telegram announcing his appointment to a government position. Something else happened that made him very proud and glad. In secret he was in the habit of writing verses and during the year before several of them had been printed in poetry magazines. One of the societies that give prizes for what they think the best poems published during the year put his name at the head of its list. The story of his triumph was printed in the newspapers of his home city and one of them also printed his picture.

As might have been expected he was excited and in a rather highly strung nervous state all during that week. Almost every evening he went to call on his fiancée, the daughter of a judge. When he got there the house was filled with people and many letters, telegrams and packages were being received. He stood a little to one side and men and women kept coming up to speak to him. They congratulated him upon his success in getting the government position and on his achievement as a poet. Everyone seemed to be praising him and when he went home and to bed he could not sleep. On Wednesday evening he went to the theatre and it seemed to him that people all over the house recognized him. Everyone nodded and smiled. After the first act five or six men and two women left their seats to gather about him. A little group was formed. Strangers sitting along the same row of seats stretched their necks and looked. He had never received so much attention before, and now a fever of expectancy took possession of him.

As he explained when he told me of his experience, it was for him an altogether abnormal time. He felt like one floating in air. When he got into bed after seeing so many people and hearing so many words of praise his head whirled round and round. When he closed his eyes a crowd of people invaded his room. It seemed as though the minds of all the people of his city were centered on himself. The most absurd fancies took possession of him. He imagined himself riding in a carriage through the streets of a city. Windows were thrown open and people ran out at the doors of houses. "There he is. That's him," they shouted, and at the words a glad cry arose. The carriage drove into a street blocked with people. A hundred thousand pairs of eyes looked up at him. "There you are! What a fellow you have managed to make of yourself!" the eyes seemed to be saying.

My friend could not explain whether the excitement of the people was due to the fact that he had written a new poem or whether, in his new government position, he had performed some notable act. The apartment where he lived at that time was on a street perched along the top of a cliff far out at the edge of his city, and from his bedroom window he could look down over trees and factory roofs to a river. As he could not sleep and as the fancies that kept crowding in upon him only made him more excited, he got out of bed and tried to think.

As would be natural under such circumstances, he tried to control his thoughts, but when he sat by the window and was wide awake a most unexpected and humiliating thing happened. The night was clear and fine. There was a moon. He wanted to dream of the woman who was to be his wife, to think out lines for noble poems, or make plans that would affect his career. Much to his surprise his mind refused to do anything of the sort.

At a corner of the street where he lived there was a small cigar store and newspaper stand run by a fat man of forty and his wife, a small active woman with bright gray eyes. In the morning he stopped there to buy a paper before going down to the city. Sometimes he saw only the fat man, but often the man had disappeared and the woman waited on him. She was, as he assured me at least twenty times in telling me his tale, a very ordinary person with nothing special or notable about her, but for some reason he could not explain, being in her presence stirred him profoundly. During that week in the midst of his distraction she was the only person he knew who stood out clear and distinct in his mind. When he wanted so much to think noble thoughts he could think only of her. Before he knew what was happening his imagination had taken hold of the notion of having a love affair with the woman.

"I could not understand myself," he declared, in telling me the story. "At night, when the city was quiet and when I should have been asleep, I thought about her all the time. After two or three days of that sort of thing the consciousness of her got into my daytime thoughts. I was terribly muddled. When I went to see the woman who is now my wife I found that my love for her was in no way affected by my vagrant thoughts. There was but one woman in the world I wanted to live with and to be my comrade in undertaking to improve my own character and my position in the world, but for the moment, you see, I wanted this other woman to be in my arms. She had worked her way into my being. On all sides people were saying I was a big man who would do big things, and there I was. That evening when I went to the theatre I walked home because I knew I would be unable to sleep, and to satisfy the annoying impulse in myself I went and stood on the sidewalk before the tobacco shop. It was a two-story building, and I knew the woman lived upstairs with her husband. For a long time I stood in the darkness with my body pressed against the wall of the building, and then I thought of the two of them up there and no doubt in bed together. That made me furious.

"Then I grew more furious with myself. I went home and got into bed, shaken with anger. There are certain books of verse and some prose writings that have always moved me deeply, and so I put several books on a table by my bed.

"The voices in the books were like the voices of the dead. I did not hear them. The printed words would not penetrate into my consciousness. I tried to think of the woman I loved, but her figure had also become something far away, something with which I for the moment seemed to have nothing to do. I rolled and tumbled about in the bed. It was a miserable experience.

"On Thursday morning I went into the store. There stood the woman alone. I think she knew how I felt. Perhaps she had been thinking of me as I had been thinking of her. A doubtful hesitating smile played about the corners of her mouth. She had on a dress made of cheap cloth and there was a tear on the shoulder. She must have been ten years older than myself. When I tried to put my pennies on the glass counter, behind which she stood, my hand trembled so that the pennies made a sharp rattling noise. When I spoke the voice that came out of my throat did not sound like anything that had ever belonged to me. It barely arose above a thick whisper. 'I want you,' I said. 'I want you very much. Can't you run away from your husband? Come to me at my apartment at seven tonight.'

"The woman did come to my apartment at seven. That morning she didn't say anything at all. For a minute perhaps we stood looking at each other. I had forgotten everything in the world but just her. Then she nodded her head and I went away. Now that I think of it I cannot remember a word I ever heard her say. She came to my apartment at seven and it was dark. You must understand this was in the month of October. I had not lighted a light and I had sent my servant away.

"During that day I was no good at all. Several men came to see me at my office, but I got all muddled up in trying to talk with them. They attributed my rattle-headedness to my approaching marriage and went away laughing.

"It was on that morning, just the day before my marriage, that I got a long and very beautiful letter from my fiancée. During the night before she also had been unable to sleep and had got out of bed to write the letter. Everything she said in it was very sharp and real, but she herself, as a living thing, seemed to have receded into the distance. It seemed to me that she was like a bird, flying far away in distant skies, and that I was like a perplexed bare-footed boy standing in the dusty road before a farm house and looking at her receding figure. I wonder if you will understand what I mean?

"In regard to the letter. In it she, the awakening woman, poured out her heart. She of course knew nothing of life, but she was a woman. She lay, I suppose, in her bed feeling nervous and wrought up as I had been doing. She realized that a great change was about to take place in her life and was glad and afraid too. There she lay thinking of it all. Then she got out of bed and began talking to me on the bit of paper. She told me how afraid she was and how glad too. Like most young women she had heard things whispered. In the letter she was very sweet and fine. 'For a long time, after we are married, we will forget we are a man and woman,' she wrote. 'We will be human beings. You must remember that I am ignorant and often I will be very stupid. You must love me and be very patient and kind. When I know more, when after a long time you have taught me the way of life, I will try to repay you. I will love you tenderly and passionately. The possibility of that is in me or I would not want to marry at all. I am afraid but I am also happy. O, I am so glad our marriage time is near at hand!'

"Now you see clearly enough what a mess I was in. In my office, after I had read my fiancée's letter, I became at once very resolute and strong. I remember that I got out of my chair and walked about, proud of the fact that I was to be the husband of so noble a woman. Right away I felt concerning her as I had been feeling about myself before I found out what a weak thing I was. To be sure I took a strong resolution that I would not be weak. At nine that evening I had planned to run in to see my fiancée. 'I'm all right now,' I said to myself. 'The beauty of her character has saved me from myself. I will go home now and send the other woman away.' In the morning I had telephoned to my servant and told him that I did not want him to be at the apartment that evening and I now picked up the telephone to tell him to stay at home.

"Then a thought came to me. 'I will not want him there in any event,' I told myself. 'What will he think when he sees a woman coming in my place on the evening before the day I am to be married?' I put the telephone down and prepared to go home. 'If I want my servant out of the apartment it is because I do not want him to hear me talk with the woman. I cannot be rude to her. I will have to make some kind of an explanation,' I said to myself.

"The woman came at seven o'clock, and, as you may have guessed, I let her in and forgot the resolution I had made. It is likely I never had any intention of doing anything else. There was a bell on my door, but she did not ring, but knocked very softly. It seems to me that everything she did that evening was soft and quiet, but very determined and quick. Do I make myself clear? When she came I was standing just within the door where I had been standing and waiting for a half hour. My hands were trembling as they had trembled in the morning when her eyes looked at me and when I tried to put the pennies on the counter in the store. When I opened the door she stepped quickly in and I took her into my arms. We stood together in the darkness. My hands no longer trembled. I felt very happy and strong.

"Although I have tried to make everything clear I have not told you what the woman I married is like. I have emphasized, you see, the other woman. I make the blind statement that I love my wife, and to a man of your shrewdness that means nothing at all. To tell the truth, had I not started to speak of this matter I would feel more comfortable. It is inevitable that I give you the impression that I am in love with the tobacconist's wife. That's not true. To be sure I was very conscious of her all during the week before my marriage, but after she had come to me at my apartment she went entirely out of my mind.

"Am I telling the truth? I am trying very hard to tell what happened to me. I am saying that I have not since that evening thought of the woman who came to my apartment. Now, to tell the facts of the case, that is not true. On that evening I went to my fiancée at nine, as she had asked me to do in her letter. In a kind of way I cannot explain the other woman went with me. This is what I mean—you see I had been thinking that if anything happened between me and the tobacconist's wife I would not be able to go through with my marriage. 'It is one thing or the other with me,' I had said to myself.

"As a matter of fact I went to see my beloved on that evening filled with a new faith in the outcome of our life together. I am afraid I muddle this matter in trying to tell it. A moment ago I said the other woman, the tobacconist's wife, went with me. I do not mean she went in fact. What I am trying to say is that something of her faith in her own desires and her courage in seeing things through went with me. Is that clear to you? When I got to my fiancée's house there was a crowd of people standing about. Some were relatives from distant places I had not seen before. She looked up quickly when I came into the room. My face must have been radiant. I never saw her so moved. She thought her letter had affected me deeply, and of course it had. Up she jumped and ran to meet me. She was like a glad child. Right before the people who turned and looked inquiringly at us, she said the thing that was in her mind. 'O, I am so happy,' she cried. 'You have understood. We will be two human beings. We will not have to be husband and wife.'

"As you may suppose everyone laughed, but I did not laugh. The tears came into my eyes. I was so happy I wanted to shout. Perhaps you understand what I mean. In the office that day when I read the letter my fiancée had written I had said to myself, 'I will take care of the dear little woman.' There was something smug, you see, about that. In her house when she cried out in that way, and when everyone laughed, what I said to myself was something like this: 'We will take care of ourselves.' I whispered something of the sort into her ears. To tell you the truth I had come down off my perch. The spirit of the other woman did that to me. Before all the people gathered about I held my fiancée close and we kissed. They thought it very sweet of us to be so affected at the sight of each other. What they would have thought had they known the truth about me God only knows!

"Twice now I have said that after that evening I never thought of the other woman at all. That is partially true but, sometimes in the evening when I am walking alone in the street or in the park as we are walking now, and when evening comes softly and quickly as it has come tonight, the feeling of her comes sharply into my body and mind. After that one meeting I never saw her again. On the next day I was married and I have never gone back into her street. Often, however, as I am walking along as I am doing now, a quick sharp earthy feeling takes possession of me. It is as though I were a seed in the ground and the warm rains of the spring had come. It is as though I were not a man but a tree.

"And now you see I am married and everything is all right. My marriage is to me a very beautiful fact. If you were to say that my marriage is not a happy one I could call you a liar and be speaking the absolute truth. I have tried to tell you about this other woman. There is a kind of relief in speaking of her. I have never done it before. I wonder why I was so silly as to be afraid that I would give you the impression I am not in love with my wife. If I did not instinctively trust your understanding I would not have spoken. As the matter stands I have a little stirred myself up. Tonight I shall think of the other woman. That sometimes occurs. It will happen after I have gone to bed. My wife sleeps in the next room to mine and the door is always left open. There will be a moon tonight, and when there is a moon long streaks of light fall on her bed. I shall awake at midnight tonight. She will be lying asleep with one arm thrown over her head.

"What is it that I am now talking about? A man does not speak of his wife lying in bed. What I am trying to say is that, because of this talk, I shall think of the other woman tonight. My thoughts will not take the form they did during the week before I was married. I will wonder what has become of the woman. For a moment I will again feel myself holding her close. I will think that for an hour I was closer to her than I have ever been to anyone else. Then I will think of the time when I will be as close as that to my wife. She is still, you see, an awakening woman. For a moment I will close my eyes and the quick, shrewd, determined eyes of that other woman will look into mine. My head will swim and then I will quickly open my eyes and see again the dear woman with whom I have undertaken to live out my life. Then I will sleep and when I awake in the morning it will be as it was that evening when I walked out of my dark apartment after having had the most notable experience of my life. What I mean to say, you understand is that, for me, when I awake, the other woman will be utterly gone."

The Kiss

[KATE CHOPIN]

It was still quite light out of doors, but inside with the curtains drawn and the smoldering fire sending out a dim, uncertain glow, the room was full of deep shadows.

Brantain sat in one of these shadows; it had overtaken him and he did not mind. The obscurity lent him courage to keep his eyes fastened as ardently as he liked upon the girl who sat in the firelight.

She was very handsome, with a certain fine, rich coloring that belongs to the healthy brune type. She was quite composed, as she idly stroked the satiny coat of the cat that lay curled in her lap, and she occasionally sent a slow glance into the shadow where her companion sat. They were talking low, of indifferent things which plainly were not the things that occupied their thoughts. She knew that he loved her—a frank, blustering fellow without guile enough to conceal his feelings, and no desire to do so. For two weeks past he had sought her society eagerly and persistently. She was confidently waiting for him to declare himself and she meant to accept him. The rather insignificant and unattractive Brantain was enormously rich; and she liked and required the entourage which wealth could give her.

During one of the pauses between their talk of the last tea and the next reception the door opened and a young man entered whom Brantain knew quite well. The girl turned her face toward him. A stride or two brought him to her side, and bending over her chair—before she could suspect his intention, for she did not realize that he had not seen her visitor—he pressed an ardent, lingering kiss upon her lips.

Brantain slowly arose; so did the girl arise, but quickly, and the newcomer stood between them, a little amusement and some defiance struggling with the confusion in his face.

"I believe," stammered Brantain, "I see that I have stayed too long. I—I had no idea—that is, I must wish you good-bye." He was clutching his hat with both hands, and probably did not perceive that she was extending her hand to him, her presence of mind had not completely deserted her; but she could not have trusted herself to speak.

"Hang me if I saw him sitting there, Nattie! I know it's deuced awkward for you. But I hope you'll forgive me this once—this very first break. Why, what's the matter?"

"Don't touch me; don't come near me," she returned angrily. "What do you mean by entering the house without ringing?"

"I came in with your brother, as I often do," he answered coldly, in self-justification. "We came in the side way. He went upstairs and I came in here hoping to find you. The explanation is simple enough and ought to satisfy you that the misadventure was unavoidable. But do say that you forgive me, Nathalie," he entreated, softening.

"Forgive you! You don't know what you are talking about. Let me pass. It depends upon—a good deal whether I ever forgive you."

At that next reception which she and Brantain had been talking about she approached the young man with a delicious frankness of manner when she saw him there.

"Will you let me speak to you a moment or two, Mr. Brantain?" she asked with an engaging but perturbed smile. He seemed extremely unhappy; but when she took his arm and walked away with him, seeking a retired corner, a ray of hope mingled with the almost comical misery of his expression. She was apparently very outspoken.

"Perhaps I should not have sought this interview, Mr. Brantain; but—but, oh, I have been very uncomfortable, almost miserable since that little encounter the other afternoon. When I thought how you might have misinterpreted it, and believed things"—hope was plainly gaining the ascendancy over misery in Brantain's round, guileless face—"Of course, I know it is nothing to you, but for my own sake I do want you to understand that Mr. Harvy is an intimate friend of long standing. Why, we have always been like cousins—like brother and sister, I may say. He is my brother's most intimate associate and often fancies that he is entitled to the same privileges as the family. Oh, I know it is absurd, uncalled for, to tell you this; undignified even," she was almost weeping, "but it makes so much difference to me what you think of— of me." Her voice had grown very low and agitated. The misery had all disappeared from Brantain's face.

"Then you do really care what I think, Miss Nathalie? May I call you Miss Nathalie?" They turned into a long, dim corridor that was lined on either side with tall, graceful plants. They walked slowly to the very end of it. When they turned to retrace their steps Brantain's face was radiant and hers was triumphant.

Harvy was among the guests at the wedding; and he sought her out in a rare moment when she stood alone.

"Your husband," he said, smiling, "has sent me over to kiss you."

A quick blush suffused her face and round polished throat. "I suppose it's natural for a man to feel and act generously on an occasion of this kind. He tells me he doesn't want his marriage to interrupt wholly that pleasant intimacy which has existed between you and me. I don't know what you've been telling him," he said with an insolent smile, "but he has sent me here to kiss you."

She felt like a chess player who, by the clever handling of his pieces, sees the game taking the course intended. Her eyes were bright and tender with a smile as they glanced up into his; and her lips looked hungry for the kiss which they invited.

"But, you know," he went on quietly, "I didn't tell him so, it would have seemed ungrateful, but I can tell you. I've stopped kissing women; it's dangerous."

Well, she had Brantain and his million left. A person can't have everything in this world; and it was a little unreasonable of her to expect it.

The Fairy Amoureuse

[EMILE ZOLA]

Do you hear the rain, Nanon, beating against the windows? And the wind sighing through the long corridor? It's a horrid night, a night when poor wretches shiver before the gates of the rich, who dance indoors in rooms bright with many gilded chandeliers. Take off those silk slippers of yours, and come sit on my knee before the blazing hearth. Lay aside your gorgeous finery: I'm going to tell you a pretty fairy tale this evening.

Once upon a time, Nanon, there stood on the top of a mountain an ancient castle, somber and forbidding to look upon. It was a mass of turrets and ramparts and portcullises with heavy clanking chains; men-at-arms clad in steel from top to toe stood guard night and day on its battlements. Of those who came to the castle only warriors found

a welcome at the hands of its master, Count
Enguerrand.

If you had seen this old warrior stalking through
the long galleries, and heard the sudden outbursts of
his dry and menacing voice, you would have trembled with fright, just like his niece Odette, a pious
and pretty little lady. Have you ever seen an Easter
daisy among the nettles and briars open its petals in
the early morning to the first kiss of the sun? Odette
was like that, living among the rough knights in
attendance on her uncle. Whenever she caught sight
of him she would suddenly stop playing, and her eyes
fill with tears. She had grown tall and fair, and often
sighed with a vague desire for she knew not what;
and every time the Lord Enguerrand appeared she
was seized with an unspeakable and growing dread.

She had her room in a turret in a distant part of
the castle, and spent her time embroidering lovely
banners; she found repose in praying to God and in
looking out of her window at the emerald landscape
and the azure sky. How often, at night, had she risen
from her bed and gone to the window to gaze at the
stars! How often had the heart of this sixteen-year-
old child leaped up toward the vasty spaces of the
heavens, asking her radiant sisters of the firmament
what it was that so troubled her! And after these
sleepless nights, these first stirrings of her yet unconscious love, she would have strange promptings urging

her to embrace the rough old knight her uncle. But a short answer or a stern glance would check her impulse, and all atremble she would take up her needle again. You are sorry, Nanon, for the poor child: she was like a fresh-scented flower whose loveliness and scent are alike spurned.

One day as poor Odette was sitting at her window following with her eyes the flight of two doves, she heard a soft voice far below her at the foot of the castle wall. She leaned out and saw a handsome young man who, with a song on his lips, demanded hospitality of the inmates of the castle. Though she listened intently, she could not understand what he said, but the sweet voice made her heart heavy, and the tears ran slowly down her cheeks, wetting the sprig of marjoram which she held in her hand.

But the castle gates were not opened, and a man-at-arms cried out from the walls:

"Stand back. Only soldiers are admitted here."

Odette continued to look out of the window. She let slip the flower from her hand, still wet with her tears. It fell near the feet of the singer who, raising his eyes and seeing the fair hair of the girl, kissed the sprig and turned away, though he stopped at every step to look back. After he had disappeared, Odette went to her prie-dieu and prayed a long time. She gave thanks to heaven, she knew not why; she felt happy, though she did not suspect the reason of her happiness. And that night she dreamed a beautiful dream. She saw again the sprig of marjoram she had thrown to the young man. Slowly, out of the midst of the quivering leaves, there emerged a tiny fairy, with flame-colored wings, a crown of myosotis, and a long robe of green, the color of hope.

"Odette," said the fairy in a soothing voice, "I am the Fairy Amoureuse. It was I who sent the young man Lois to you this morning—the young man with the enchanting voice. It was I who, seeing your tears, wanted to dry them. I go about the world seeking lonely hearts and bringing together those who sigh in solitude. I visit the peasant's hut as well as the lord's manor, and at times I see fit to unite the shepherd's crook with the king's scepter. I sow flowers under the feet of those I protect. I enthrall them with bonds so precious and sweet that their hearts throb with joy. My home is among the green things that grow, the forest paths, and in wintertime among the glowing logs on the hearth, in the rooms of husbands and wives. Wherever I set my foot there are kisses and tenderness. Cry no more, Odette, I am Amoureuse, the good Fairy, who have come to dry your tears."

Then she disappeared again into her flower, which closed once more and became an ordinary bud.

You know, of course, Nanon, that the Fairy Amoureuse really exists. Watch her dancing in our own home, and pity the poor people who don't believe in her.

When Odette awoke next morning a ray of sunshine lighted up her room, the song of a bird rose to her high tower and the morning breeze, scented with the first kiss of the flowers, caressed her bright tresses. She rose, happy, and spent the whole day singing, hoping that the Fairy's prophecy would come true. Sometimes she would scan the countryside, smiling at each swiftly flying bird, and feeling within her breast something that made her happy and forced her to clap her hands with joy.

When evening came she descended into the great hall. Near the Count Enguerrand was a knight who listened respectfully to what the old man was saying. Odette seated herself before the fireplace, where a cricket was chirping, and busily plied her ivory distaff.

As she worked, she cast glances from time to time at the stranger knight, and once she caught sight of the sprig of marjoram, which he held tight in one hand. By that sign, and by his sweet voice, she recognized Lois. She almost cried aloud for joy, but in order to conceal her blushes she leaned forward toward the glowing logs, and shook the fire with a long iron rod. The flames darted upwards in a brilliant array, and all at once out of the shower of sparks the Fairy Amoureuse sprang up smiling. Shaking from her green silk robe the bits of burning wood that looked like grains of pure gold, she made off into the great hall where, invisible to the Count, she stood just behind the two young people, while the old warrior went on busily relating the details of a frightful battle with the Infidels. The Fairy spoke in a soothing undertone:

"You must love each other, my children. Leave to the old the memories of youth, and the telling of long tales by the fireside. Let your kisses be the only sound to mingle with the crackling logs. Later will be time enough to mitigate the sorrows of old age by remembering the happy hours long past. When you love at sixteen, words are of no avail: a single look tells more than a lengthy discourse. Love each other, my children, and let old age prate."

Then she covered the two with her wings so completely that the Count, who was explaining how the Giant Buch the Iron-headed was killed by a great blow from the hand of Giralda of the Heavy Sword, could not see when Lois implanted his first kiss on the brow of the trembling Odette.

Now I must tell you, Nanon, about those beautiful wings of the Fairy Amoureuse. They were as transparent as glass and as delicate as the wings of a fly. But when two lovers are in danger of being seen, they grow and grow and become so thick and so opaque that they shut off the view of anything behind them and prevent anyone's hearing the kisses. And so the old man went on and on with his wondrous tale, while Lois continued to caress the fair Odette, right in the presence of the wicked old lord.

Good heavens, what wonderful wings they were! Young girls, I am told, discover them for themselves, and more than one has succeeded in concealing herself from her grandparents. Isn't that so, Nanon?

Well, when the Count had at last brought to a close his lengthy discourse, the Fairy Amoureuse disappeared again into the fire, and Lois withdrew after thanking his host and throwing a farewell kiss to Odette. The girl was so happy that she dreamed that night of mountains studded with flowers made bright by millions of stars, each of them a thousand times more radiant than the sun.

Next morning she went down into the garden, wandering from arbor to arbor. In one of them she came upon a man-at-arms, bowed to him and was about to pass on, when she noticed a sprig of marjoram in his hand, still wet with tears, and recognized again her Lois. He had come to the castle under a new disguise. He made her sit down on a grassy bank near a fountain, and they gazed into each other's eyes, delighted to be able to see each other's features by the light of day. The warblers sang, and the two lovers felt that the Fairy Amoureuse must surely be hovering about in the air near them.

I shan't tell you all that the discreet old oak trees heard that morning. It was pleasant to watch the boy and the girl sitting there chatting hour after hour, so long indeed that one warbler found ample time to build herself a nest in a nearby bush.

Suddenly the heavy footsteps of Count Enguer-rand were heard in the garden walk. The lovers trembled, but the water of the fountain rippled more sweetly than ever, and Amoureuse rose out of the crystal stream, a smile on her face. She covered the lovers with her wings, and quickly slipped between them and the Count, who was greatly surprised to hear voices and yet see no one at all.

Holding her friends in her embrace, she repeated to them in a soft undertone:

"I am she who protects love, who closes the eyes and ears of those who no longer love. Fear nothing, dear lovers: love each other in this beautiful clear sunlight, in these garden walks, by the side of these fountains, wherever you happen to be. I am with you, watching over you. God has sent me among men, and they who scoff at sacred things shall never interrupt you. God gave me these beautiful wings, telling me, 'Go, and let the hearts of the young rejoice!' Love each other, while I keep guard over you."

Then she darted off, gathering dew off the foliage (her only nourishment), and taking with her in her joyous round Odette and Lois, whose arms were ever interlaced.

You will ask me what the lovers did next? Really, my dear, I hardly dare tell you. I'm afraid you would not believe me, or be jealous of *their* happiness, and refuse to return my kisses. Naughty girl, you are curious, aren't you? I see I shall have to satisfy your curiosity.

Know then, that the Fairy flew hither and thither until nightfall, and when she tried to separate her lovers, she found them so reluctant that she had to give them a good talking-to. It seems (for her voice was low) that she said things so beautiful that their faces lighted up and their eyes opened wide from happiness. And after she had done speaking and they consented to her proposal, she touched their foreheads with her magic wand.

Suddenly—oh, Nanon, how big your eyes are! And how you would tap your little foot if I were to refuse to tell you the sequel! Suddenly, Lois and Odette were changed into stalks of marjoram, so large and magnificent that only a fairy could have made them so. There they were, side by side, so close that their leaves were entwined. Marvelous flowers they were; they would bloom forever, and eternally mingle their perfumes and their dew.

As for the Count Enguerrand, they say he consoled himself by relating every single night the story of the Giant Buch the Iron-Headed and how he was killed by a great blow from the hand of Giralda of the Heavy Sword.

And now, Nanon, when we go to the country, we shall look for the two magic marjorams and ask them in which flower we may find the Fairy Amoureuse. Perhaps, my dear, there is a little moral hidden in this tale. However, I have told it to you here, as we sit stretched out before the hearth, just in order to make you forget the December rain beating against our windows, and in the hope that it will inspire you to love a little more the young man who told it to you.

A Modern Cinderella: or, The Little Old Shoe

[LOUISA MAY ALCOTT]

HOW IT WAS LOST

Among green New England hills stood an ancient house, many-gabled, mossy-roofed, and quaintly built, but picturesque and pleasant to the eye; for a brook ran babbling through the orchard that encompassed it about, a garden-plot stretched upward to the whispering birches on the slope, and patriarchal elms stood sentinel upon the lawn, as they had stood almost a century ago, when the Revolution rolled that way and found them young.

One summer morning, when the air was full of country sounds, of mowers in the meadow, blackbirds by the brook, and the low of the kine upon the hillside, the old house wore its cheeriest aspect, and a certain humble history began.

"Nan!"

"Yes, Di."

And a head, brown-locked, blue-eyed, soft-featured, looked in at the open door in answer to the call.

"Just bring me the third volume of *Wilhelm Meister*—there's a dear. It's hardly worth while to rouse such a restless ghost as I, when I'm once fairly laid."

As she spoke, Di pushed up her black braids, thumped the pillow of the couch where she was lying, and with eager eyes went down the last page of her book.

"Nan!"

"Yes, Laura," replied the girl, coming back with the third volume for the literary cormorant, who took it with a nod, still too intent upon the "Confessions of a Fair Saint" to remember the failings of a certain plain sinner.

"Don't forget the Italian cream for dinner. I depend upon it; for it's the only thing fit for me this hot weather."

And Laura, the cool blonde, disposed the folds of her white gown more gracefully about her, and touched up the eyebrow of the Minerva she was drawing.

"Little daughter!"

"Yes, father."

"Let me have plenty of clean collars in my bag, for I must go at three; and some of you bring me a glass of cider in about an hour—I shall be in the lower garden."

The old man went away into his imaginary paradise, and Nan into that domestic purgatory on a summer day—the kitchen. There were vines about the windows, sunshine on the floor, and order everywhere; but it was haunted by a cooking-stove, that family altar whence such varied incense rises to appease the appetite of household gods, before which such dire incantations are pronounced to ease the wrath and woe of the priestess of the fire, and about which often linger saddest memories of wasted temper, time, and toil.

Nan was tired, having risen with the birds—hurried, having many cares those happy little housewives never know—and disappointed in a hope that hourly "dwindled, peaked, and pined." She was too young to make the anxious lines upon her forehead seem at home there, too patient to be burdened with the labor others should have shared, too light of heart to be pent up when earth and sky were keeping a blithe holiday. But she was one of that meek sisterhood who, thinking humbly of themselves, believe they are honored by being spent in the service of less conscientious souls, whose careless thanks seem quite reward enough.

To and fro she went, silent and diligent, giving the grace of willingness to every humble or distasteful task the day had brought her; but some malignant

sprite seemed to have taken possession of her kingdom, for rebellion broke out everywhere. The kettles
would boil over most obstreperously—the mutton
refused to cook with the meek alacrity to be expected
from the nature of a sheep—the stove, with unnecessary warmth of temper, would glow like a fiery
furnace—the irons would scorch—the linens would
dry—and spirits would fail, though patience never.

Nan tugged on, growing hotter and wearier, more
hurried and more hopeless, till at last the crisis
came; for in one fell moment she tore her gown,
burnt her hand, and smutched the collar she was
preparing to finish in the most unexceptionable
style. Then, if she had been a nervous woman, she
would have scolded; being a gentle girl, she only
"lifted up her voice and wept."

"Behold, she watereth her linen with salt tears, and
bewaileth herself because of much tribulation. But,
lo! help cometh from afar: a strong man bringeth
lettuce wherewith to stay her, plucketh berries to
comfort her withal, and clasheth cymbals that she
may dance for joy."

The voice came from the porch, and, with her hope
fulfilled, Nan looked up to greet John Lord, the
house-friend, who stood there with a basket on his
arm; and as she saw his honest eyes, kind lips, and help-
ful hands, the girl thought this plain young man the
comeliest, most welcome sight she had beheld that day.

"How good of you, to come through all this heat, and not to laugh at my despair!" she said, looking up like a grateful child, as she led him in.

"I only obeyed orders, Nan; for a certain dear old lady had a motherly presentiment that you had got into a domestic whirlpool, and sent me as a sort of life-preserver. So I took the basket of consolation, and came to fold my feet upon the carpet of contentment in the tent of friendship."

As he spoke, John gave his own gift in his mother's name, and bestowed himself in the wide window-seat, where morning glories nodded at him, and the old butternut sent pleasant shadows dancing to and fro.

His advent, like that of Orpheus in Hades, seemed to soothe all unpropitious powers with a sudden spell. The fire began to slacken, the kettles began to lull, the meat began to cook, the irons began to cool, the clothes began to behave, the spirits began to rise, and the collar was finished off with most triumphant success. John watched the change, and, though a lord of creation, abased himself to take compassion on the weaker vessel, and was seized with a great desire to lighten the homely tasks that tried her strength of body and soul. He took a comprehensive glance about the room; then, extracting a dish from the closet, proceeded to imbrue his hands in the straw-berries' blood.

"Oh, John, you needn't do that; I shall have time when I've turned the meat, made the pudding, and done these things. See, I'm getting on finely now— you're a judge of such matters; isn't that nice?"

As she spoke, Nan offered the polished absurdity for inspection with innocent pride.

"Oh that I were a collar, to sit upon that hand!" sighed John—adding argumentatively, "As to the berry question, I might answer it with a gem from Dr. Watts, relative to 'Satan' and 'idle hands,' but will merely say, that as a matter of public safety, you'd better leave me alone; for such is the destructiveness of my nature, that I shall certainly eat something hurtful, break something valuable, or sit upon something crushable, unless you let me concentrate my energies by knocking off these young fellows' hats, and preparing them for their doom."

Looking at the matter in a charitable light, Nan consented, and went cheerfully on with her work, wondering how she could have thought ironing an infliction, and been so ungrateful for the blessings of her lot.

"Where's Sally?" asked John, looking vainly for the energetic functionary who usually pervaded that region like a domestic policewoman, a terror to cats, dogs, and men.

"She has gone to her cousin's funeral, and won't be back till Monday. There seems to be a great fatality among her relations; for one dies, or comes to grief in some way, about once a month. But I don't blame poor Sally for wanting to get away from this place now and then. I think I could find it in my heart to murder an imaginary friend or two, if I had to stay here long.

And Nan laughed so blithely, it was a pleasure to hear her.

"Where's Di?" asked John, seized with a most unmasculine curiosity all at once.

"She is in Germany with *Wilhelm Meister*; but, though 'lost to sight, to memory dear'; for I was just thinking, as I did her things, how clever she is to like all kinds of books that I don't understand at all, and to write things that make me cry with pride and delight. Yes, she's a talented dear, though she hardly knows a needle from a crowbar, and will make herself one great blot some of these days, when the 'divine afflatus' descends upon her, I'm afraid."

And Nan rubbed away with sisterly Zeal at Di's forlorn hose and inky pocket-handkerchiefs.

"Where is Laura?" proceeded the inquisitor.

"Well, I might say that she was in Italy; for she is copying some fine thing of Raphael's, or Michel Angelo's, or some great creature's or other; and she looks so picturesque in her pretty gown, sitting before her easel, that it's really a sight to behold, and I've peeped two or three times to see how she gets on."

And Nan bestirred herself to prepare the dish wherewith her picturesque sister desired to prolong her artistic existence.

"Where is your father?" John asked again, checking off each answer with a nod and a little frown.

"He is down in the garden, deep in some plan about melons, the beginning of which seems to consist in stamping the first proposition in Euclid all over the bed, and then poking a few seeds into the middle of each. Why, bless the dear man! I forgot it was time for the cider. Wouldn't you like to take it to him, John? He'd love to consult you; and the lane is so cool, it does one's heart good to look at it."

John glanced from the steamy kitchen to the shadowy path, and answered with a sudden assumption of immense industry—"I couldn't possibly go, Nan—I've so much on my hands. You'll have to do it yourself. 'Mr. Robert of Lincoln' has something for your private ear; and the lane is so cool, it will do one's heart good to see you in it. Give my regards to your father, and, in the words of 'Little Mabel's' mother, with slight variations—

> 'Tell the dear old body
> This day I cannot run,
> For the pots are boiling over
> And the mutton isn't done.'"

"I will; but please, John, go in to the girls and be comfortable; for I don't like to leave you here," said Nan.

"You insinuate that I should pick at the pudding or invade the cream, do you? Ungrateful girl, leave me!" And, with melodramatic sternness, John extinguished her in his broad-brimmed hat, and offered the glass like a poisoned goblet.

Nan took it, and went smiling away. But the lane might have been the desert of Sahara, for all she knew of it; and she would have passed her father as unconcernedly as if he had been an apple tree, had he not called out—"Stand and deliver, little woman!"

She obeyed the venerable highwayman, and followed him to and fro, listening to his plans and directions with a mute attention that quite won his heart.

"That hop-pole is really an ornament now, Nan; this sage bed needs weeding—that's good work for you girls; and, now I think of it, you'd better water the lettuce in the cool of the evening, after I'm gone."

To all of which remarks Nan gave her assent; though the hop-pole took the likeness of a tall figure she had seen in the porch, the sage-bed, curiously enough, suggested a strawberry ditto, the lettuce vividly reminded her of certain vegetable productions a basket had brought, and the bob-o-link only sung in his cheeriest voice, "Go home, go home! he is there!"

She found John—he having made a freemason of himself, by assuming her little apron—meditating over the partially spread table, lost in amaze at its desolate appearance; one half its proper paraphernalia having been forgotten, and the other half put on awry. Nan laughed till the tears ran over her cheeks, and John was gratified at the efficacy of his treatment; for her face had brought a whole harvest of sunshine from the garden, and all her cares seemed to have been lost in the windings of the lane.

"Nan, are you in hysterics?" cried Di, appearing, book in hand. "John, you absurd man, what are you doing?"

"I'm helpin' the maid of all work, please marm." And John dropped a curtsy with his limited apron.

Di looked ruffled, for the merry words were a covert reproach; and with her usual energy of manner and freedom of speech she tossed "Wilhelm" out of the window, exclaiming, irefully—

"That's always the way; I'm never where I ought to be, and never think of anything till it's too late; but it's all Goethe's fault. What does he write books full of smart 'Phillinas' and interesting 'Meisters' for? How can I be expected to remember that Sally's away, and people must eat, when I'm hearing the 'Harper' and little 'Mignon'? John, how dare you come here and do my work, instead of shaking me and telling me to do it myself? Take that toasted child away, and fan her like a Chinese mandarin, while I dish up this dreadful dinner."

John and Nan fled like chaff before the wind, while Di, full of remorseful Zeal, charged at the kettles, and wrenched off the potatoes' jackets, as if she were revengefully pulling her own hair. Laura had a vague intention of going to assist; but, getting lost among the lights and shadows of Minerva's helmet, forgot to appear till dinner had been evoked from chaos and peace was restored.

At three o'clock, Di performed the coronation-ceremony with her father's best hat; Laura re-tied his old-fashioned neck cloth, and arranged his white locks with an eye to saintly effect; Nan appeared with a beautifully written sermon, and suspicious ink stains on the fingers that slipped it into his pocket; John attached himself to the bag; and the patriarch was escorted to the door of his tent with the triumphal procession which usually attended his out-goings and in-comings. Having kissed the female portion of his tribe, he ascended the venerable chariot, which received him with audible lamentation, as its rheumatic joints swayed to and fro.

"Good-bye, my dears! I shall be back early on Monday morning; so take care of yourselves, and be sure you all go and hear Mr. Emerboy preach to-morrow. My regards to your mother, John. Come, Solon!"

But Solon merely cocked one ear, and remained a fixed fact; for long experience had induced the philosophic beast to take for his motto the Yankee maxim, "Be sure you're right, then go ahead!" He knew things were not right; therefore he did not go ahead.

"Oh, by the way, girls, don't forget to pay Tommy Mullein for bringing up the cow: he expects it tonight. And, Di, don't sit up till daylight, nor let Laura stay out in the dew. Now, I believe, I'm off. Come, Solon!"

But Solon only cocked the other ear, gently agitated his mortified tail, as premonitory symptoms of departure, and never stirred a hoof, being well aware that it always took three "comes" to make a "go."

"Bless me! I've forgotten my spectacles. They are probably shut up in that volume of Herbert on my table. Very awkward to find myself without them ten miles away. Thank you, John. Don't neglect to water the lettuce, Nan, and don't overwork yourself, my little 'Martha.' Come—"

At this juncture, Solon suddenly went off, like "Mrs. Gamp," in a sort of walking swoon, apparently deaf and blind to all mundane matters, except the refreshments awaiting him ten miles away; and the benign old pastor disappeared, humming "Hebron" to the creaking accompaniment of the bulgy chaise.

Laura retired to take her siesta; Nan made a small *carbonaro* of herself by sharpening her sister's crayons, and Di, as a sort of penance for past sins, tried her patience over a piece of knitting, in which she soon originated a somewhat remarkable pattern, by dropping every third stitch, and seaming ad libitum. If John had been a gentlemanly creature, with refined tastes, he would have elevated his feet and made a nuisance of himself by indulging in a "weed"; but being only an uncultivated youth, with a rustic regard for pure air and womankind in general, he kept his head uppermost, and talked like a man, instead of smoking like a chimney.

"It will probably be six months before I sit here again, tangling your threads and maltreating your needles, Nan. How glad you must feel to hear it!" he said, looking up from a thoughtful examination of the hard-working little citizens of the Industrial Community settled in Nan's workbasket.

"No, I'm very sorry; for I like to see you coming and going as you used to, years ago, and I miss you very much when you are gone, John," answered truthful Nan, whittling away in a sadly wasteful manner, as her thoughts flew back to the happy times when a little lad rode a little lass in the big wheel-barrow, and never split his load—when two brown heads bobbed daily side by side to school, and the favorite play was *Babes in the Wood*, with Di for a somewhat peckish robin to cover the small martyrs with any vegetable substance that lay at hand. Nan sighed, as she thought of these things, and John regarded the battered thimble on his fingertip with increased benignity of aspect as he heard the sound.

"When are you going to make your fortune, John, and get out of that disagreeable hardware concern?" demanded Di, pausing after an exciting "round," and looking almost as much exhausted as if it had been a veritable pugilistic encounter.

"I intend to make it by plunging still deeper into 'that disagreeable hardware concern'; for, next year, if the world keeps rolling, and John Lord is alive, he will become a partner, and then—and then—"

The color sprang up into the young man's cheek, his eyes looked out with a sudden shine, and his hand seemed involuntarily to close, as if he saw and seized some invisible delight.

"What will happen then, John?" asked Nan, with a wondering glance.

"I'll tell you in a year, Nan—wait till then." And John's strong hand unclosed, as if the desired good were not to be his yet.

Di looked at him, with a knitting-needle stuck into her hair, saying, like a sarcastic unicorn: "I really thought you had a soul above pots and kettles, but I see you haven't; and I beg your pardon for the injustice I have done you."

Not a whit disturbed, John smiled, as if at some mighty pleasant fancy of his own, as he replied: "Thank you, Di; and as a further proof of the utter depravity of my nature, let me tell you that I have the greatest possible respect for those articles of ironmongery. Some of the happiest hours of my life have been spent in their society; some of my pleasantest associations are connected with them; some of my best lessons have come to me from among them; and when my fortune is made, I intend to show my gratitude by taking three flat-irons rampant for my coat of arms."

Nan laughed merrily, as she looked at the burns on her hand; but Di elevated the most prominent feature of her brown countenance, and sighed despondingly: "Dear, dear, what a disappointing world this is! I no sooner build a nice castle in Spain, and settle a smart young knight therein, than down it comes about my ears; and the ungrateful youth, who might fight dragons, if he chose, insists on quenching his energies in a saucepan, and making a Saint Lawrence of himself by wasting his life on a series of gridirons. Ah, if I were only a man, I would do something better than that, and prove that heroes are not all dead yet. But, instead of that, I'm only a woman, and must sit rasping my temper with absurdities like this." And Di wrestled with her knitting as if it were Fate, and she were paying off the grudge she owed it.

John leaned toward her, saying, with a look that made his plain face handsome.

"Di, my father began the world as I begin it, and left it the richer for the useful years he spent here—as I hope I may leave it some half-century hence. His memory makes that dingy shop a pleasant place to me; for there he made an honest name, led an honest life, and bequeathed to me his reverence for honest work. That is a sort of hardware, Di, that no rust can corrupt, and which will always prove a better fortune than any your knights can achieve with sword and shield. I think I am not quite a clod, or quite without some aspirations above money-getting; for I sincerely desire that courage which makes daily life heroic by self-denial and cheerfulness of heart; I am eager to conquer my own rebellious nature, and earn the confidence of innocent and upright souls; I have a great ambition to become as good a man and leave as green a memory behind me as old John Lord."

Di winked violently, and seamed five times in perfect silence; but quiet Nan had the gift of knowing when to speak, and by a timely word saved her sister from a thundershower and her stocking from destruction.

"John, have you seen Philip since you wrote about your last meeting with him?"

The question was for John, but the soothing tone was for Di, who gratefully accepted it, and perked up again with speed.

"Yes; and I meant to have told you about it," answered John, plunging into the subject at once. "I saw him a few days before I came home, and found him more disconsolate than ever—'just ready to go to the Devil,' as he forcibly expressed himself. I consoled the poor lad as well as I could, telling him his wisest plan was to defer his proposed expedition, and go on as steadily as he had begun—thereby proving the injustice of your father's prediction concerning his want of perseverance, and the sincerity of his affection. I told him the change in Laura's health and spirits was silently working in his favor, and that a few more months of persistent endeavor would conquer your father's prejudice against him, and make him a stronger man for the trial and the pain. I read him bits about Laura from your own and Di's letters, and he went away at last as patient as Jacob, ready to serve another 'seven years' for his beloved Rachel."

"God bless you for it, John!" cried a fervent voice; and, looking up, they saw the cold, listless Laura transformed into a tender girl, all aglow with love and longing, as she dropped her mask, and showed a living countenance eloquent with the first passion and softened by the first grief of her life.

John rose involuntarily in the presence of an innocent nature whose sorrow needed no interpreter to him. The girls read sympathy in his brotherly regard, and found comfort in the friendly voice that asked, half playfully, half seriously, "Shall I tell him that he is not forgotten, even for an Apollo? that Laura the artist has not conquered Laura the woman? and predict that the good daughter will yet prove the happy wife?"

With a gesture full of energy, Laura tore her Minerva from top to bottom, while two great tears rolled down the cheeks grown wan with hope deferred.

"Tell him I believe all things, hope all things, and that I never can forget."

Nan went to her and held her fast, leaving the prints of two loving, but grimy hands upon her shoulders; Di looked on approvingly, for, though rather stony-hearted regarding the cause, she fully appreciated the effect; and John, turning to the window, received the commendations of a robin swaying on an elm-bough with sunshine on its ruddy breast.

The clock struck five, and John declared that he must go; for, being an old-fashioned soul, he fancied that his mother had a better right to his last hour than any younger woman in the land—always remembering that "she was a widow, and he her only son."

Nan ran away to wash her hands, and came back with the appearance of one who had washed her face also: and so she had; but there was a difference in the water.

"Play I'm your father, girls, and remember it will be six months before 'that John' will trouble you again."

With which preface the young man kissed his former playfellows as heartily as the boy had been wont to do, when stern parents banished him to distant schools, and three little maids bemoaned his fate. But times were changed now; for Di grew alarmingly rigid during the ceremony; Laura received the salute like a grateful queen; and Nan returned it with heart and eyes and tender lips, making such an improvement on the childish fashion of the thing, that John was moved to support his paternal character by softly echoing her father's words: "Take care of yourself, my little 'Martha.'"

Then they all streamed after him along the garden path, with the endless messages and warnings girls are so prone to give; and the young man, with a great softness at his heart, went away, as many another John has gone, feeling better for the companionship of innocent maidenhood, and stronger to wrestle with temptation, to wait and hope and work.

"Let's throw a shoe after him for luck, as dear old 'Mrs. Gummage' did after 'David' and the 'willin' Barkis!' Quick, Nan! you always have old shoes on; toss one, and shout, 'Good luck!'" cried Di, with one of her eccentric inspirations.

Nan tore off her shoe, and threw it far along the dusty road, with a sudden longing to become that auspicious article of apparel, that the omen might not fail.

Looking backward from the hilltop, John answered the meek shout cheerily, and took in the group with a lingering glance: Laura in the shadow of the elms, Di perched on the fence, and Nan leaning far over the gate with her hand above her eyes and the sunshine touching her brown hair with gold. He waved his hat and turned away; but the music seemed to die out of the blackbird's song, and in all the summer landscape his eye saw nothing but the little figure at the gate.

"Bless and save us! here's a flock of people coming; my hair is in a toss, and Nan's without her shoe; run! fly, girls! or the Philistines will be upon us!" cried Di, tumbling off her perch in sudden alarm.

Three agitated young ladies, with flying draperies and countenances of mingled mirth and dismay, might have been seen precipitating themselves into a respectable mansion with unbecoming haste; but the squirrels were the only witnesses of this "vision of sudden flight," and, being used to ground-and-loft tumbling, didn't mind it.

When the pedestrians passed, the door was decorously closed, and no one visible but a young man who snatched something out of the road, and marched away again, whistling with more vigor of tone than accuracy of tune, "Only that, and nothing more."

HOW IT WAS FOUND

Summer ripened into autumn, and something fairer than

> *Sweet-peas and mignonette*
> *In Annie's garden grew.*

Her nature was the counterpart of the hillside grove, where as a child she had read her fairy tales, and now as a woman turned the first pages of a more wondrous legend still. Lifted above the many gabled roof, yet not cut off from the echo of human speech, the little grove seemed a green sanctuary, fringed about with violets, and full of summer melody and bloom. Gentle creatures haunted it, and there was none to make afraid; wood-pigeons cooed and crickets chirped their shrill roundelays, anemones and lady-ferns looked up from the moss that kissed the wanderer's feet. Warm airs were all afloat, full of vernal odors for the grateful sense, silvery birches shimmered like spirits of the wood, larches gave their green tassels to the wind, and pines made airy music sweet and solemn, as they stood looking heavenward through veils of summer sunshine or shrouds of wintry snow.

Nan never felt alone now in this charmed wood; for when she came into its precincts, once so full of solitude, all things seemed to wear one shape, familiar eyes looked at her from the violets in the grass, familiar words sounded in the whisper of the leaves, and she grew conscious that an unseen influence filled the air with new delights, and touched earth and sky with a beauty never seen before. Slowly these May-flowers budded in her maiden heart, rosily they bloomed, and silently they waited till some lover of such lovely herbs should catch their fresh aroma, should brush away the fallen leaves, and lift them to the sun.

Though the eldest of the three, she had long been overtopped by the more aspiring maids. But though she meekly yielded the reins of government, when-ever they chose to drive, they were soon restored to her again; for Di fell into literature, and Laura into love. Thus engrossed, these two forgot many duties which even bluestockings and *innamoratas* are expected to perform, and slowly all the homely humdrum cares that housewives know became Nan's daily life, and she accepted it without a thought of discontent. Noiseless and cheerful as the sunshine, she went to and fro, doing the tasks that mothers do, but without a mother's sweet reward, holding fast the numberless slight threads that bind a household tenderly together, and making each day a beautiful success.

Di, being tired of running, riding, climbing, and boating, decided at last to let her body rest and put her equally active mind through what classical collegians term "a course of sprouts." Having undertaken to read and know everything, she devoted herself to the task with great energy, going from Sue to Swedenborg with perfect impartiality, and having different authors as children have sundry distempers, being fractious while they lasted, but all the better for them when once over. Carlyle appeared like scarlet fever, and raged violently for a time; for, being anything but a "passive bucket," Di became prophetic with Mahomet, belligerent with Cromwell, and made the French Revolution a veritable Reign of Terror to her family. Goethe and Schiller alternated like fever and ague; Mephistopheles became her hero, Joan of Arc her model, and she turned her black eyes red over Egmont and Wallenstein. A mild attack of Emerson followed, during which she was lost in a fog, and her sisters rejoiced inwardly when she emerged informing them that

> *The Sphinx was drowsy,*
> *Her wings were furled.*

Poor Di was floundering slowly to her proper place; but she splashed up a good deal of foam by getting out of her depth, and rather exhausted herself by trying to drink the ocean dry.

Laura, after the "midsummer night's dream" that often comes to girls of seventeen woke up to find that youth and love were no match for age and common sense. Philip had been flying about the world like a thistledown for five-and-twenty years, generous-hearted, frank, and kind, but with never an idea of the serious side of life in his handsome head. Great, therefore, were the wrath and dismay of the enamored thistledown, when the father of his love mildly objected seeing her begin the world in a balloon with a very tender but very inexperienced aeronaut for a guide.

"Laura is too young to 'play house' yet, and you are too unstable to assume the part of lord and master, Philip. Go and prove that you have prudence, patience, energy, and enterprise, and I will give you my girl—but not before. I must seem cruel, that I may be truly kind; believe this, and let a little pain lead you to great happiness, or show you where you would have made a bitter blunder."

The lovers listened, owned the truth of the old man's words, bewailed their fate, and—yielded—Laura for love of her father, Philip for love of her. He went away to build a firm foundation for his castle in the air, and Laura retired into an invisible convent, where she cast off the world, and regarded her sympathizing sisters through a grate of superior knowledge and unsharable grief. Like a devout nun, she worshipped "St. Philip," and firmly believed in his miraculous powers. She fancied that her woes set her apart from common cares, and slowly fell into a dreamy state, professing no interest in any mundane matter, but the art that first attracted Philip. Crayons, bread-crusts, and gray paper became glorified in Laura's eyes and her one pleasure was to sit pale and still before her easel, day after day, filling her portfolios with the faces he had once admired. Her sisters observed that every Bacchus, Piping Faun, or Dying Gladiator bore some likeness to a comely countenance that heathen god or hero never owned; and seeing this, they privately rejoiced that she had found such solace for her grief.

Mrs. Lord's keen eye had read a certain newly written page in her son's heart—his first chapter of that romance, begun in Paradise, whose interest never flags, whose beauty never fades, whose end can never come till Love lies dead. With womanly skill she divined the secret, with motherly discretion she counseled patience, and her son accepted her advice, feeling, that, like many a healthful herb, its worth lay in its bitterness.

"Love like a man, John, not like a boy, and learn to know yourself before you take a woman's happiness into your keeping. You and Nan have known each other all your lives; yet, till this last visit, you never thought you loved her more than any other childish friend. It is too soon to say the words so often spoken hastily—so hard to be recalled. Go back to your work, dear, for another year; think of Nan in the light of this new hope; compare her with comelier, gayer girls; and by absence prove the truth of your belief. Then, if distance only makes her dearer, if time only strengthens your affection, and no doubt of your own worthiness disturbs you, come back and offer her what any woman should be glad to take— my boy's true heart."

John smiled at the motherly pride of her words, but answered with a wistful look.

"It seems very long to wait, mother. If I could just ask her for a word of hope, I could be very patient then."

"Ah, my dear, better bear one year of impatience now than a lifetime of regret hereafter. Nan is happy; why disturb her by a word which will bring the tender cares and troubles that come soon enough to such conscientious creatures as herself? If she loves you, time will prove it; therefore let the new affection spring and ripen as your early friendship has done, and it will be all the stronger for a summer's growth. Philip was rash, and has to bear his trial now, and Laura shares it with him. Be more generous, John; make your trial, bear your doubts alone, and give Nan the happiness without the pain. Promise me this, dear—promise me to hope and wait."

The young man's eye kindled, and in his heart there rose a better chivalry, a truer valor, than any Di's knights had ever known.

"I'll try, mother," was all he said; but she was satisfied, for John seldom tried in vain.

"Oh, girls, how splendid you are!" It does my heart good to see my handsome sisters in their best array," cried Nan, one mild October night as she put the last touches to certain airy raiment fashioned by her own skillful hands, and then fell back to survey the grand effect.

Di and Laura were preparing to assist at an "event of the season," and Nan, with her own locks fallen on her shoulders, for want of sundry combs promoted to her sisters' heads, and her dress in unwonted disorder, for lack of the many pins extracted in exciting crises of the toilet, hovered like an affectionate bee about two very full-blown flowers.

"Laura looks like a cool Undine, with the ivy-wreaths in her shining hair; and Di has illuminated herself to such an extent with those scarlet leaves, that I don't know what great creature she resembles most," said Nan, beaming with sisterly admiration.

"Like Juno, Zenobia, and Cleopatra simmered into one, with a touch of Xantippe by way of spice. But, to my eye, the finest woman of the three is the disheveled young person embracing the bed-post; for she stays at home herself and gives her time and taste to making homely people fine—which is a waste of good material, and an imposition on the public."

As Di spoke, both the fashion plates looked affectionately at the gray-gowned figure; but, being works of art, they were obliged to nip their feelings in the bud, and reserve their caresses till they returned to common life.

"Put on your bonnet, and we'll leave you at Mrs. Lord's on our way. It will do you good, Nan; and perhaps there may be news from John," added Di, as she bore down upon the door like a man-of-war under full sail.

"Or from Philip," sighed Laura, with a wistful look.

Whereupon Nan persuaded herself that her strong inclination to sit down was owing to want of exercise, and the heaviness of her eyelids a freak of imagination; so, speedily smoothing her ruffled plumage, she ran down to tell her father of the new arrangement.

"Go, my dear, by all means. I shall be writing; and you will be lonely, if you stay. But I must see my girls; for I caught glimpses of certain surprising phantoms flitting by the door."

Nan led the way, and the two pyramids revolved before him with the rigidity of lay-figures, much to the good man's edification; for with his fatherly pleasure there was mingled much mild wonderment at the amplitude of the array.

"Yes, I see my geese are really swans, though there is such a cloud between us that I feel a long way off, and hardly know them. But this little daughter is always available, always my 'cricket on the hearth.'"

As he spoke, her father drew Nan closer, kissed her tranquil face, and smiled content.

"Well, if ever I see picters, I see 'em now, and I declare to goodness it's as interestin' as play-actin', every bit. Miss Di, with all them boughs in her head, looks like the Queen of Sheby, when she went a-visitin' What's-his-name; and if Miss Laura a'n't as sweet as a lally-barster figger, I should like to know what is."

In her enthusiasm, Sally gamboled about the girls, flourishing her milk-pan like a modern Miriam about to sound her timbrel for excess of joy.

Laughing merrily, the two Mont Blancs bestowed themselves in the family ark, Nan hopped up beside Patrick, and Solon, roused from his lawful slumbers, morosely trundled them away. But, looking backward with a last "Good night!" Nan saw her father still standing at the door with smiling countenance, and the moonlight falling like a benediction on his silver hair.

"Betsey shall go up the hill with you, my dear, and here's a basket of eggs for your father. Give him my love, and be sure you let me know the next time he is poorly," Mrs. Lord said, when her guest rose to depart after an hour of pleasant chat.

But Nan never got the gift; for, to her great dismay, her hostess dropped the basket with a crash, and flew across the room to meet a tall shape pausing in the shadow of the door. There was no need to ask who the newcomer was; for, even in his mother's arms, John looked over her shoulder with an eager nod to Nan, who stood among the ruins with never a sign of weariness in her face, nor the memory of a care at her heart—for they all went out when John came in.

"Now tell us how and why and when you came. Take off your coat, my dear! And here are the old slippers. Why didn't you let us know you were coming so soon? How have you been? and what makes you so late to-night? Betsey, you needn't put on your bonnet. And—oh, my dear boy, have you been to supper yet?"

Mrs. Lord was a quiet soul, and her flood of questions was purred softly in her son's ear; for, being a woman, she must talk, and being a mother, must pet the one delight of her life, and make a little festival when the lord of the manor came home. A whole drove of fatted calves were metaphorically killed, and a banquet appeared with speed.

John was not one of those romantic heroes who can go through three volumes of hairbreadth escapes without the faintest hint of that blessed institution, dinner; therefore, like "Lady Leatherbridge," he "partook copiously of everything," while the two women beamed over each mouthful with an interest that enhanced its flavor, and urged upon him cold meat and cheese, pickles and pie, as if dyspepsia and nightmare were among the lost arts.

Then he opened his budget of news and fed them.

"I was coming next month, according to custom; but Philip fell upon and so tempted me, that I was driven to sacrifice myself to the cause of friendship, and up we came tonight. He would not let me come here till we had seen your father, Nan; for the poor lad was pining for Laura, and hoped his good behavior for the past year would satisfy his judge and secure his recall. We had a fine talk with your father; and, upon my life, Phil seemed to have received the gift of tongues, for he made a most eloquent plea, which I've stored away for future use, I assure you. The dear old gentleman was very kind, told Phil he was satisfied with the success of his probation, that he should see Laura when he liked, and, if all went well, should receive his reward in the spring. It must be a delightful sensation to know you have made a fellow-creature happy as those words made Phil tonight."

John paused, and looked musingly at the matronly teapot, as if he saw a wondrous future in its shine.

Nan twinkled off the drops that rose at the thought of Laura's joy, and said, with grateful warmth: "You say nothing of your own share in the making of that happiness, John; but we know it, for Philip has told Laura in his letter all that you have been to him, and I am sure there was other eloquence beside his own before father granted all you say he has. Oh, John, I thank you very much for this!"

Mrs. Lord beamed a whole midsummer of delight upon her son, as she saw the pleasure these words gave him, though he answered simply:

"I only tried to be a brother to him, Nan; for he has been most kind to me. Yes, I said my little say tonight, and gave my testimony in behalf of the prisoner at the bar, a most merciful judge pronounced his sentence, and he rushed straight to Mrs. Leigh's to tell Laura the blissful news. Just imagine the scene when he appears, and how Di will open her wicked eyes and enjoy the spectacle of the disheveled lover, the bride-elect's tears, the stir, and the romance of the thing. She'll cry over it tonight, and caricature it tomorrow."

And John led the laugh at the picture he had conjured up, to turn the thoughts of Di's dangerous sister from himself.

At ten Nan retired into the depths of her old bonnet with a far different face from the one she brought out of it, and John, resuming his hat, mounted guard.

"Don't stay late, remember, John!" And in Mrs. Lord's voice there was a warning tone that her son interpreted aright.

"I'll not forget, mother."

And he kept his word; for though Philip's happiness floated temptingly before him, and the little figure at his side had never seemed so dear, he ignored the bland winds, the tender night, and set a seal upon his lips, thinking manfully within himself, "I see many signs of promise in her happy face; but I will wait and hope a little longer for her sake."

"Where is father, Sally?" asked Nan, as that functionary appeared, blinking owlishly, but utterly repudiating the idea of sleep.

"He went down the garding, miss, when the gentlemen cleared, bein' a little flustered by the goin's on. Shall I fetch him in?" asked Sally, as irreverently as if her master were a bag of meal.

"No, we will go ourselves." And slowly the two paced down the leaf-strewn walk.

Fields of yellow grain were waving on the hillside, and sere corn-blades rustled in the wind, from the orchard came the scent of ripening fruit, and all the garden plots lay ready to yield up their humble offerings to their master's hand. But in the silence of the night a greater Reaper had passed by, gathering in the harvest of a righteous life, and leaving only tender memories for the gleaners who had come so late.

The old man sat in the shadow of the tree his own hands planted; its fruitful boughs shone ruddily, and its leaves still whispered the low lullaby that hushed him to his rest.

"How fast he sleeps! Poor father! I should have come before and made it pleasant for him."

As she spoke, Nan lifted up the head bent down upon his breast, and kissed his pallid cheek.

"Oh, John, this is not sleep!"

"Yes, dear, the happiest he will ever know."

For a moment the shadows flickered over three white faces and the silence deepened solemnly. Then John reverently bore the pale shape in, and Nan dropped down beside it, saying, with a rain of grateful years:

"He kissed me when I went, and said a last 'good night!'"

For an hour steps went to and fro about her, many voices whispered near her, and skillful hands touched the beloved clay she held so fast; but one by one the busy feet passed out, one by one the voices died away, and human skill proved vain. Then Mrs. Lord drew the orphan to the shelter of her arms, soothing her with the mute solace of that motherly embrace.

"Nan, Nan! here's Philip! come and see!"

The happy call reechoed through the house, and Nan sprang up as if her time for grief were past.

"I must tell them. Oh, my poor girls, how will they bear it?—they have known so little sorrow!"

But there was no need for her to speak; other lips had spared her the hard task. For, as she stirred to meet them, a sharp cry rent the air, steps rang upon the stairs, and the two wild-eyed creatures came into the hush of that familiar room, for the first time meeting with no welcome from their father's voice.

With one impulse, Di and Laura fled to Nan, and the sisters clung together in a silent embrace, far more eloquent than words. John took his mother by the hand, and led her from the room, closing the door upon the sacredness of grief.

"Yes, we are poorer than we thought; but when everything is settled, we shall get on very well. We can let a part of this great house, and live quietly together until spring; then Laura will be married, and Di can go on their travels with them, as Philip wishes her to do. We shall be cared for; so never fear for us, John."

Nan said this, as her friend parted from her a week later, after the saddest holiday he had ever known.

"And what becomes of you, Nan?" he asked, watching the patient eyes that smiled when others would have wept.

"I shall stay in the dear old house; for no other place would seem like home to me. I shall find some little child to love and care for, and be quite happy till the girls come back and want me."

John nodded wisely, as he listened, and went away prophesying within himself: "She shall find something more than a child to love; and, God willing, shall be very happy till the girls come home and—cannot have her."

Nan's plan was carried into effect. Slowly the divided waters closed again, and the three fell back into their old life. But the touch of sorrow drew them closer; and, though invisible, a beloved presence still moved among them, a familiar voice still spoke to them in the silence of their softened hearts. Thus the soil was made ready, and in the depth of winter the good seed was sown, was watered with many tears, and soon sprang up green with the promise of a harvest for their after years.

Di and Laura consoled themselves with their favorite employments, unconscious that Nan was growing paler, thinner, and more silent, as the weeks went by, till one day she dropped quietly before them, and it suddenly became manifest that she was utterly worn out with many cares and the secret suffering of a tender heart bereft of the paternal love which had been its strength and stay.

"I'm only tired, dear girls. Don't be troubled, for I shall be up tomorrow," she said cheerily, as she looked into the anxious faces bending over her.

But the weariness was of many months' growth, and it was weeks before that "tomorrow" came.

Laura installed herself as a nurse, and her devotion was repaid fourfold; for, sitting at her sister's bedside, she learned a finer art than that she had left. Her eye grew clear to see the beauty of a self-denying life, and in the depths of Nan's meek nature she found the strong, sweet virtues that made her what she was.

Then remembering that these womanly attributes were a bride's best dowry, Laura gave herself to their attainment, that she might become to another household the blessing Nan had been to her own; and turning from the worship of the goddess Beauty, she gave her hand to that humbler and more human teacher, Duty—learning her lessons with a willing heart, for Philip's sake.

Di corked her inkstand, locked her bookcase, and went at housework as if it were a five-barred gate; of course she missed the leap, but scrambled bravely through, and appeared much sobered by the exercise. Sally had departed to sit under a vine and fig-tree of her own, so Di had undisputed sway; but if dishpans and dusters had tongues, direful would have been the history of that crusade against frost and fire, indolence and inexperience. But they were dumb, and Di scorned to complain, though her struggles were pathetic to behold, and her sisters went through a series of messes equal to a course of "Prince Benreddin's" peppery tarts. Reality turned Romance out of doors; for, unlike her favorite heroines in satin and tears, or helmet and shield, Di met her fate in a big checked apron and dust-cap, wonderful to see; yet she wielded her broom as stoutly as "Moll Pitcher" shouldered her gun, and marched to her daily martyrdom in the kitchen with as heroic a heart as the "Maid of Orleans" took to her stake.

Mind won the victory over matter in the end, and Di was better all her days for the tribulations and the triumphs of that time; for she drowned her idle fancies in her wash-tub, made burnt-offerings of selfishness and pride, and learned the worth of self-denial, as she sang with happy voice among the pots and kettles of her conquered realm.

Nan thought of John, and in the stillness of her sleepless nights prayed Heaven to keep him safe, and make her worthy to receive and strong enough to bear the blessedness or pain of love.

Snow fell without, and keen winds howled among the leafless elms, but "herbs of grace" were blooming beautifully in the sunshine of sincere endeavor, and this dreariest season proved the most fruitful of the year; for love taught Laura, labor chastened Di, and patience fitted Nan for the blessing of her life.

Nature, that stillest, yet most diligent of housewives, began at last that "spring-cleaning" which she makes so pleasant that none find the heart to grumble as they do when other matrons set their premises a-dust. Her handmaids, wind and rain and sun, swept, washed, and garnished busily, green carpets were unrolled, apple-boughs were hung with draperies of bloom, and dandelions, pet nurslings of the year, came out to play upon the sward.

From the South returned that opera troupe whose manager is never in despair, whose tenor never sulks, whose prima donna never fails, and in the orchard bona fide matinees were held, to which buttercups and clovers crowded in their prettiest spring hats and verdant young blades twinkled their dewy lorgnettes, as they bowed and made way for the floral belles.

May was bidding June good-morrow, and the roses were just dreaming that it was almost time to wake, when John came again into the quiet room, which now seemed the Eden that contained his Eve. Of course there was a jubilee; but something seemed to have befallen the whole group, for never had they all appeared in such odd frames of mind. John was restless, and wore an excited look, most unlike his usual serenity of aspect.

Nan the cheerful had fallen into a well of silence and was not to be extracted by any hydraulic power, though she smiled like the June sky over her head. Di's peculiarities were out in full force, and she looked as if she would go off like a torpedo at a touch; but through all her moods there was a half-triumphant, half-remorseful expression in the glance she fixed on John. And Laura, once so silent, now sang like a blackbird, as she flitted to and fro; but her fitful song was always, "Philip, my king."

John felt that there had come a change upon the three, and silently divined whose unconscious influence had wrought the miracle. The embargo was off his tongue, and he was in a fever to ask that question which brings a flutter to the stoutest heart; but though the "man" had come, the "hour" had not. So, by way of steadying his nerves, he paced the room, pausing often to take notes of his companions, and each pause seemed to increase his wonder and content.

He looked at Nan. She was in her usual place, the rigid little chair she loved, because it once was large enough to hold a curly-headed playmate and herself. The old work-basket was at her side, and the battered thimble busily at work; but her lips wore a smile they had never worn before, the color of the unblown roses touched her cheek, and her downcast eyes were full of light.

He looked at Di. The inevitable book was on her knee, but its leaves were uncut; the strong-minded knob of hair still asserted its supremacy aloft upon her head, and the triangular jacket still adorned her shoulders in defiance of all fashions, past, present, or to come; but the expression of her brown countenance had grown softer, her tongue had found a curb, and in her hand lay a card with "Potts, Kettel, & Co." inscribed thereon, which she regarded with never a scornful word for the "Co."

He looked at Laura. She was before her easel, as of old; but the pale nun had given place to a blooming girl, who sang at her work, which was no prim Pallas, but a Clytie turning her human face to meet the sun.

"John, what are you thinking of?"

He stirred as if Di's voice had disturbed his fancy at some pleasant pastime, but answered with his usual sincerity.

"I was thinking of a certain dear old fairy tale called 'Cinderella.'"

"Oh!" said Di; and her "Oh" was a most impressive monosyllable. "I see the meaning of your smile now; and though the application of the story is not very complimentary to all parties concerned, it is very just and very true."

She paused a moment, then went on with softened voice and earnest mien:

"You think I am a blind and selfish creature. So I am, but not so blind and selfish as I have been; for many tears have cleared my eyes, and much sincere regret has made me humbler than I was. I have found a better book than any father's library can give me, and I have read it with a love and admiration that grew stronger as I turned the leaves. Henceforth I take it for my guide and gospel, and, looking back upon the selfish and neglectful past, can only say, Heaven bless your dear heart, Nan!"

Laura echoed Di's last words; for, with eyes as full of tenderness, she looked down upon the sister she had lately learned to know, saying, warmly, "Yes,

'Heaven bless your dear heart, Nan!' I never can forget all you have been to me; and when I am far away
with Philip, there will always be one countenance
more beautiful to me than any pictured face I may
discover, there will be one place more dear to me
than Rome. The face will be yours, Nan—always so
patient, always so serene; and the dearer place will be
this home of ours, which you have made so pleasant
to me all these years by kindnesses as numberless and
noiseless as the drops of dew."

"Dear girls, what have I ever done, that you
should love me so?" cried Nan, with happy wonderment, as the tall heads, black and golden, bent to
meet the lowly brown one, and her sisters' mute lips
answered her.

Then Laura looked up, saying, playfully, "Here are
the good and wicked sisters—where shall we find
the Prince?"

"There!" cried Di, pointing to John; and then her
secret went off like a rocket; for, with her old
impetuosity she said, "I have found you out, John,
and am ashamed to look you in the face, remembering the past. Girls, you know, when father died, John
sent us money, which he said Mr. Owen had long
owed us and had paid at last? It was a kind lie, John,
and a generous thing to do; for we needed it, but
never would have taken it as a gift. I know you meant
that we should never find this out; but yesterday I

met Mr. Owen returning from the West, and when I thanked him for a piece of justice we had not expected of him, he gruffly told me he had never paid the debt, never meant to pay it, for it was out-lawed, and we could not claim a farthing. John, I have laughed at you, thought you stupid, treated you unkindly; but I know you now, and never shall forget the lesson you have taught me. I am proud as Lucifer, but I ask you to forgive me, and I seal my real repentance so—and so."

With tragic countenance, Di rushed across the room, threw both arms about the astonished young man's neck and dropped an energetic kiss upon his cheek. There was a momentary silence; for Di finely illustrated her strong-minded theories by crying like the weakest of her sex. Laura, with "the ruling pas-sion strong in death," still tried to draw, but broke her pet crayon, and endowed her Clytie with a supple-mentary orb, owing to the dimness of her own. And Nan sat with drooping eyes, that shone upon her work, thinking with tender pride:

"They know him now, and love him for his gener-ous heart."

Di spoke first, rallying to her colors though a little daunted by her loss of self-control.

"Don't laugh, John—I couldn't help it; and don't think I'm not sincere, for I am—I am; and I will prove it by growing good enough to be your friend.

That debt must all be paid, and I shall do it; for I'll turn my books and pen to some account, and write stories full of dear old souls like you and Nan; and some one, I know, will like and buy them, though they are not 'works of Shakespeare.' I've thought of this before, have felt I had the power in me; now I have the motive, and now I'll do it."

If Di had proposed to translate the Koran, or build a new Saint Paul's, there would have been many chances of success; for, once moved, her will, like a battering-ram, would knock down the obstacles her wits could not surmount. John believed in her most heartily, and showed it, as he answered, looking into her resolute face:

"I know you will, and yet make us very proud of our 'Chaos,' Di. Let the money lie, and when you have made a fortune, I'll claim it with enormous interest; but, believe me, I feel already doubly repaid by the esteem so generously confessed, so cordially bestowed, and can only say, as we used to years ago— 'Now let's forgive and forget.'"

But proud Di would not let him add to her obligation, even by returning her impetuous salute; she slipped away, and, shaking off the last drops, answered with a curious mixture of old freedom and new respect.

"No more sentiment, please, John. We know each other now; and when I find a friend, I never let him go. We have smoked the pipe of peace; so let us go back to our wigwams and bury the feud. Where were we when I lost my head? and what were we talking about?"

"Cinderella and the Prince."

As he spoke, John's eye kindled, and turning, he looked down at Nan, who sat diligently ornamenting with microscopic stitches a great patch going on, the wrong side out.

"Yes—so we were; and now taking pussy for the godmother, the characters of the story are well personated—all but the slipper," said Di, laughing, as she thought of the many times they had played it together years ago.

A sudden movement stirred John's frame, a sudden purpose shone in his countenance, and a sudden change befell his voice, as he said, producing from some hiding-place a little worn-out shoe.

"I can supply the slipper—who will try it first?"

Di's black eyes opened wide, as they fell on the familiar object; then her romance-loving nature saw the whole plot of that drama which needs but two to act it. A great delight flushed up into her face, as she promptly took her cue, saying:

"No need for us to try it, Laura; for it wouldn't fit us, if our feet were as small as Chinese dolls'—our parts are played out; therefore 'Exeunt wicked sisters to the music of the wedding-bells.'" And pouncing upon the dismayed artist she swept her out and closed the door with a triumphant bang.

John went to Nan, and, dropping on his knee as reverently as the herald of the fairy tale, he asked, still smiling but with lips grown tremulous:

"Will Cinderella try the little shoe, and—if it fits—go with the Prince?"

But Nan only covered up her face, weeping happy tears, while all the weary work strayed down upon the floor, as if it knew her holiday had come.

John drew the hidden face still closer, and while she listened to his eager words, Nan heard the beating of the strong man's heart, and knew it spoke the truth.

"Nan, I promised mother to be silent till I was sure I loved you wholly—sure that the knowledge would give no pain when I should tell it, as I am trying to tell it now. This little shoe has been my comforter through this long year, and I have kept it as other lovers keep their fairer favors. It has been a talisman more eloquent to me than flower or ring; for, when I saw how worn it was, I always thought of the willing feet that came and went for others' comfort all day long; when I saw the little bow you tied, I always thought to the hands so diligent in serving any one who knew a want or felt a pain; and when I recalled the gentle creature who had worn it last, I always saw her patient, tender, and devout—and tried to grow more worthy of her, that I might one day dare to ask if she would walk beside me all my life and be my 'angel in the house.' Will you, dear? Believe me, you shall never know a weariness of grief I have the power to shield you from."

Then Nan, as simple in her love as in her life, laid her arms about his neck, her happy face against his own, and answered softly:

"Oh, John, I never can be sad or tired any more!"

Mr. and Mrs. Dove

[KATHERINE MANSFIELD]

Of course he knew—no man better—that he hadn't a ghost of a chance, he hadn't an earthly. The very idea of such a thing was preposterous. So preposterous that he'd perfectly understand it if her father—well, whatever her father chose to do he'd perfectly understand. In fact, nothing short of desperation, nothing short of the fact that this was positively his last day in England for God knows how long, would have screwed him up to it. And even now. . . He chose a tie out of the chest of drawers, a blue and cream check tie, and sat on the side of his bed. Supposing she replied, "What impertinence!" would he be surprised? Not in the least, he decided, turning up his soft collar and turning it down over the tie. He expected her to say something like that. He didn't see, if he looked at the affair dead soberly, what else she could say.

Here he was! And nervously he tied a bow in front of the mirror, jammed his hair down with both hands, pulled out the flaps of his jacket pockets. Making between 500 and 600 pounds a year on a fruit farm in—of all places—Rhodesia. No capital. Not a penny coming to him. No chance of his income increasing for at least four years. As for looks and all that sort of thing, he was completely out of the running. He couldn't even boast of top-hole health, for the East Africa business had knocked him out so thoroughly that he'd had to take six months' leave. He was still fearfully pale—worse even than usual this afternoon, he thought, bending forward and peering into the mirror. Good heavens! What had happened? His hair looked almost bright green. Dash it all, he hadn't green hair at all events. That was a bit too steep. And then the green light trembled in the glass; it was the shadow from the tree outside. Reggie turned away, took out his cigarette case, but remembering how the mater hated him to smoke in his bedroom, put it back again and drifted over to the chest of drawers. No, he was dashed if he could think of one blessed thing in his favor, while she. . . Ah. . . He stopped dead, folded his arms, and leaned hard against the chest of drawers.

And in spite of her position, her father's wealth, the fact that she was an only child and far and away

the most popular girl in the neighborhood; in spite
of her beauty and her cleverness—cleverness!—it
was a great deal more than that, there was really
nothing she couldn't do; he fully believed, had it
been necessary, she would have been a genius at anything—in spite of the fact that her parents adored
her, and she them, and they'd as soon let her go all
that way as. . . In spite of every single thing you
could think of, so terrific was his love that he
couldn't help hoping. Well, was it hope? Or was this
queer, timid longing to have the chance of looking
after her, of making it his job to see that she had
everything she wanted, and that nothing came near
her that wasn't perfect—just love? How he loved
her! He squeezed hard against the chest of drawers
and murmured to it, "I love her, I love her!" And just
for the moment he was with her on the way to
Umtali. It was night. She sat in a corner asleep. Her
soft chin was tucked into her soft collar, her gold-
brown lashes lay on her cheeks. He doted on her
delicate little nose, her perfect lips, her ear like a
baby's, and the gold-brown curl that half covered it.
They were passing through the jungle. It was warm
and dark and far away. Then she woke up and said,
"Have I been asleep?" and he answered, "Yes. Are
you all right? Here, let me—" And he leaned forward to. . . He bent over her. This was such bliss that
he could dream no further. But it gave him the

courage to bound downstairs, to snatch his straw hat from the hall, and to say as he closed the front door, "Well, I can only try my luck, that's all."

But his luck gave him a nasty jar, to say the least, almost immediately. Promenading up and down the garden path with Chinny and Biddy, the ancient Pekes, was the mater. Of course Reginald was fond of the mater and all that. She——she meant well, she had no end of grit, and so on. But there was no denying it, she was rather a grim parent. And there had been moments, many of them, in Reggie's life, before Uncle Alick died and left him the fruit farm, when he was convinced that to be a widow's only son was about the worst punishment a chap could have. And what made it rougher than ever was that she was positively all that he had. She wasn't only a combined parent, as it were, but she had quarreled with all her own and the governor's relations before Reggie had won his first trouser pockets. So that whenever Reggie was homesick out there, sitting on his dark veranda by starlight, while the gramophone cried, "Dear, what is Life but Love?" his only vision was of the mater, tall and stout, rustling down the garden path, with Chinny and Biddy at her heels. . .

The mater, with her scissors outspread to snap the head of a dead something or other, stopped at the sight of Reggie.

"You are not going out, Reginald?" she asked, see-ing that he was.

"I'll be back for tea, mater," said Reggie weakly, plunging his hands into his jacket pockets.

Snip. Off came a head. Reggie almost jumped.

"I should have thought you could have spared your mother your last afternoon," said she.

Silence. The Pekes stared. They understood every word of the mater's. Biddy lay down with her tongue poked out; she was so fat and glossy she looked like a lump of half-melted toffee. But Chinny's porcelain eyes gloomed at Reginald, and he sniffed faintly, as though the whole world were one unpleasant smell. Snip, went the scissors again. Poor little beggars; they were getting it!

"And where are you going, if your mother may ask?" asked the mater.

It was over at last, but Reggie did not slow down until he was out of sight of the house and halfway to Colonel Proctor's. Then only he noticed what a top-hole afternoon it was. It had been raining all the morning, late summer rain, warm, heavy, quick, and now the sky was clear, except for a long tail of little clouds, like ducklings, sailing over the forest. There was just enough wind to shake the last drops off the trees; one warm star splashed on his hand. *Ping!*— another drummed on his hat. The empty road gleamed, the hedges smelled of briar, and how big and bright the hollyhocks glowed in the cottage gardens. And here was Colonel Proctor's—here it was already. His hand was on the gate, his elbow jogged the syringa bushes, and petals and pollen scattered over his coat sleeve. But wait a bit. This was too quick altogether. He'd meant to think the whole thing out again. Here, steady. But he was walking up the path, with the huge rose bushes on either side. It can't be done like this. But his hand had grasped the bell, given it a pull, and started it pealing wildly, as if he'd come to say the house was on fire. The house-maid must have been in the hall, too, for the front door flashed open, and Reggie was shut in the empty drawing room before that confounded bell had stopped ringing. Strangely enough, when it did, the big room, shadowy, with some one's parasol lying on top of the grand piano, bucked him up—or rather, excited him. It was so quiet, and yet in one moment the door would open, and his fate be decided. The feeling was not unlike that of being at the dentist's; he was almost reckless. But at the same time, to his immense surprise, Reggie heard himself saying, "Lord, Thou knowest, Thou hast not done much for me. . ." That pulled him up; that made him realize again how dead serious it was. Too late. The door handle turned. Anne came in, crossed the shadowy space between them, gave him her hand, and said, in her small, soft voice, "I'm so sorry, father is out. And mother is having a day in town, hat-hunting. There's only me to entertain you, Reggie."

Reggie gasped, pressed his own hat to his jacket buttons, and stammered out, "As a matter of fact, I've only come. . . to say good-bye."

"Oh!" cried Anne softly—she stepped back from him and her gray eyes danced—"what a very short visit!"

Then, watching him, her chin tilted, she laughed outright, a long, soft peal, and walked away from him over to the piano, and leaned against it, playing with the tassel of the parasol.

"I'm so sorry," she said, "to be laughing like this. I don't know why I do. It's just a bad ha—habit." And suddenly she stamped her gray shoe, and took a pocket-handkerchief out of her white woolly jacket. "I really must conquer it, it's too absurd," said she.

"Good heavens, Anne," cried Reggie, "I love to hear you laughing! I can't imagine anything more—"

But the truth was, and they both knew it, she wasn't always laughing; it wasn't really a habit. Only ever since the day they'd met, ever since that very first moment, for some strange reason that Reggie wished to God he understood, Anne had laughed at him. Why? It didn't matter where they were or what they were talking about. They might begin by being as serious as possible, dead serious—at any rate, as far as he was concerned—but then suddenly, in the middle of a sentence, Anne would glance at him, and a little quick quiver passed over her face. Her lips parted, her eyes danced, and she began laughing.

Another queer thing about it was, Reggie had an idea she didn't herself know why she laughed. He had seen her turn away, frown, suck in her cheeks, press her hands together. But it was no use. The long, soft peal sounded, even while she cried, "I don't know why I'm laughing." It was a mystery. . .

Now she tucked the handkerchief away.

"Do sit down," said she. "And smoke, won't you? There are cigarettes in that little box beside you. I'll have one too." He lighted a match for her, and as she bent forward he saw the tiny flame glow in the pearl ring she wore. "It is tomorrow that you're going, isn't it?" said Anne.

"Yes, tomorrow as ever was," said Reggie, and he blew a little fan of smoke. Why on earth was he so nervous? Nervous wasn't the word for it.

"It's—it's frightfully hard to believe," he added.

"Yes—isn't it?" said Anne softly, and she leaned forward and rolled the point of her cigarette round the green ashtray. How beautiful she looked like that!—simply beautiful—and she was so small in that immense chair. Reginald's heart swelled with tenderness, but it was her voice, her soft voice, that made him tremble. "I feel you've been here for years," she said.

Reginald took a deep breath of his cigarette. "It's ghastly, this idea of going back," be said.

"*Coo-roo-coo-coo-coo,*" sounded from the quiet.

"But you're fond of being out there, aren't you?" said Anne. She hooked her finger through her pearl necklace. "Father was saying only the other night how lucky he thought you were to have a life of your own." And she looked up at him. Reginald's smile was rather wan. "I don't feel fearfully lucky," he said lightly.

"*Roo-coo-coo-coo,*" came again. And Anne murmured, "You mean it's lonely."

"Oh, it isn't the loneliness I care about," said Reginald, and he stumped his cigarette savagely on the green ashtray. "I could stand any amount of it, used to like it even. It's the idea of—" Suddenly, to his horror, he felt himself blushing.

"*Roo-coo-coo-coo! Roo-coo-coo-coo!*"

Anne jumped up. "Come and say good-bye to my doves," she said. "They've been moved to the side veranda. You do like doves, don't you, Reggie?"

"Awfully," said Reggie, so fervently that as he opened the French window for her and stood to one side, Anne ran forward and laughed at the doves instead.

To and fro, to and fro over the fine red sand on the floor of the dove house, walked the two doves. One was always in front of the other. One ran forward, uttering a little cry, and the other followed, solemnly bowing and bowing. "You see," explained Anne, "the one in front, she's Mrs. Dove. She looks at Mr. Dove and gives that little laugh and runs forward, and he follows her, bowing and bowing. And that makes her laugh again. Away she runs, and after her," cried Anne, and she sat back on her heels, "comes poor Mr. Dove, bowing and bowing. . . and that's their whole life. They never do anything else, you know." She got up and took some yellow grains out of a bag on the roof of the dove house. "When you think of them, out in Rhodesia, Reggie, you can be sure that is what they will be doing. . ."

Reggie gave no sign of having seen the doves or of having heard a word. For the moment he was conscious only of the immense effort it took to tear his secret out of himself and offer it to Anne. "Anne, do you think you could ever care for me?" It was done. It was over. And in the little pause that followed Reginald saw the garden open to the light, the blue quivering sky, the flutter of leaves on the veranda poles, and Anne turning over the grains of maize on her palm with one finger. Then slowly she shut her hand, and the new world faded as she murmured slowly, "No, never in that way." But he had scarcely time to feel anything before she walked quickly away, and he followed her down the steps, along the garden path, under the pink rose arches, across the lawn. There, with the gay herbaceous border behind her, Anne faced Reginald. "It isn't that I'm not awfully fond of you," she said. "I am. But"— her eyes widened—"not in the way"—a quiver passed over her face—"one ought to be fond of—" Her lips parted, and she couldn't stop herself. She began laughing. "There, you see, you see," she cried, "it's your check t-tie. Even at this moment, when one would think one really would be solemn, your tie reminds me fearfully of the bow tie that cats wear in pictures! Oh, please forgive me for being so horrid, please!"

Reggie caught hold of her little warm hand. "There's no question of forgiving you," he said quickly. "How could there be? And I do believe I know why I make you laugh. It's because you're so far above me in every way that I am somehow ridiculous. I see that, Anne. But if I were to—"

"No, no." Anne squeezed his hand hard. "It's not that. That's all wrong. I'm not far above you at all. You're much better than I am. You're marvelously unselfish and. . . and kind and simple. I'm none of those things. You don't know me. I'm the most awful character," said Anne. "Please don't interrupt. And besides, that's not the point. The point is"—she shook her head—"I couldn't possibly marry a man I laughed at. Surely you see that. The man I marry—" breathed Anne softly. She broke off. She drew her hand away, and looking at Reggie she smiled strangely, dreamily. "The man I marry—"

And it seemed to Reggie that a tall, handsome, brilliant stranger stepped in front of him and took his place—the kind of man that Anne and he had seen often at the theatre, walking on to the stage from nowhere, without a word catching the heroine in his arms, and after one long, tremendous look, carrying her off to anywhere. . .

Reggie bowed to his vision. "Yes, I see," he said huskily.

Do you?" said Anne. "Oh, I do hope you do. Because I feel so horrid about it. It's so hard to explain. You know I've never—" She stopped. Reggie looked at her. She was smiling. "Isn't it funny?" she said. "I can say anything to you. I always have been able to from the very beginning."

He tried to smile, to say, "I'm glad." She went on. "I've never known anyone I like as much as I like you. I've never felt so happy with anyone. But I'm sure it's not what people and what books mean when they talk about love. Do you understand? Oh, if you only knew how horrid I feel. But we'd be like. . . like Mr. and Mrs. Dove."

That did it. That seemed to Reginald final, and so terribly true that he could hardly bear it. "Don't drive it home," he said, and he turned away from Anne and looked across the lawn. There was the gardener's cottage, with the dark ilex tree beside it. A wet, blue thumb of transparent smoke hung above the chimney. It didn't look real. How his throat ached! Could he speak? He had a shot. "I must be getting along home," he croaked, and he began walking across the lawn. But Anne ran after him. "No, don't. You can't go yet," she said imploringly. "You can't possibly go away feeling like that." And she stared up at him frowning, biting her lip.

"Oh, that's all right," said Reggie, giving himself a shake. "I'll. . . I'll—" And he waved his hand as much to say, "get over it."

"But this is awful," said Anne. She clasped her hands and stood in front of him. "Surely you do see how fatal it would be for us to marry, don't you?"

"Oh, quite, quite," said Reggie, looking at her with haggard eyes.

"How wrong, how wicked, feeling as I do. I mean, it's all very well for Mr. and Mrs. Dove. But imagine that in real life—imagine it!"

"Oh, absolutely," said Reggie, and he started to walk on. But again Anne stopped him. She tugged at his sleeve, and to his astonishment, this time, instead of laughing, she looked like a little girl who was going to cry.

"Then why, if you understand, are you so un-unhappy?" she wailed. "Why do you mind so fearfully? Why do you look so aw-awful?"

Reggie gulped, and again he waved something away. "I can't help it," he said, "I've had a blow. If I cut off now, I'll be able to——"

"How can you talk of cutting off now?" said Anne scornfully. She stamped her foot at Reggie; she was crimson. "How can you be so cruel? I can't let you go until I know for certain that you are just as happy as you were before you asked me to marry you. Surely you must see that, it's so simple."

But it did not seem at all simple to Reginald. It seemed impossibly difficult.

"Even if I can't marry you, how can I know that you're all that way away, with only that awful mother to write to, and that you're miserable, and that it's all my fault?"

"It's not your fault. Don't think that. It's just fate." Reggie took her hand off his sleeve and kissed it. "Don't pity me, dear little Anne," he said gently. And this time he nearly ran, under the pink arches, along the garden path.

"Roo-coo-coo-coo! Roo-coo-coo-coo!" sounded from the veranda. "Reggie, Reggie," from the garden.

He stopped, he turned. But when she saw his timid, puzzled look, she gave a little laugh.

"Come back, Mr. Dove," said Anne. And Reginald came slowly across the lawn.

A Sweet Day

[A D A   C A M B R I D G E]

L ord Thomas de Bohun had been married twice—and more. In fact, he was sick and tired of womenkind. And that is why he came out to Australia. He thought a year or two of travel in a savage country, free of all the trammels of civilization, would give him a rest. Besides, the second Lady Thomas had been rather nice to him, and she had died pathetically, and he missed her. Wherefore he loathed the British matchmaker for the present, and was glad to get as far away from her as possible.

He was not a roué and a reprobate, such as this introduction might imply. Nothing of the sort. A better natured or more charming young man—he was on the right side of forty still—was not to be found in London. But he was the son of a duke, poor fellow, with a great deal of money, and no work to do—misfortunes for which the fair-minded reader will make a large allowance.

In the beginning, Australia did not quite answer his expectations. Whereas he had imagined a dress-suit to be a thing unknown, he found himself obliged to wear one nightly, and he was just as ducal in our city clubs and drawing-rooms as he would have been at home—indeed, a great deal more so. But as soon as he escaped into the country he was all right. Clad in moleskins and a Crimean shirt, with a soft felt hat on his head, and big spurs on his heels, he galloped about at kangaroo hunts and cattle musters, a simple bushman of the bush (while his servant played the gentleman in Melbourne), enjoying health and happiness and the unrivaled charm of novelty to a degree unknown before. Anybody could get him who had no right to get him. The great country houses, flattering themselves that they alone could entertain him suitably, found it a most difficult matter to drop salt on his elusive tail.

He was at a bush hotel one evening, spending a convivial hour with perfect strangers, who did not know he was Lord Thomas. Having heard his name was De Bohun, they called him Mr. Bone, and were quite satisfied with that. So was he. The talk turned upon agricultural machinery, as used by English and Australian farmers respectively; and a member of the latter class, as Lord Thomas supposed, was most anxious to show him a five-furrow plough and various modern implements—American "notions" of the laborsaving kind.

"You come home with me," said the jolly old man, "and you shall see 'em working. Now do, Mr. Bone. Pot-luck, you know, but a hearty welcome."

Lord Thomas jumped at the chance, for, amongst other delightfully novel pursuits, he had set himself to the improvement of his mind in these matters, as a responsible landlord and potential duke.

"But your family?" he objected. "Would it not inconvenience them to receive a stranger without warning, and at so late an hour?"

"Not a bit of it, Mr. Bone. There's always a bed ready for anybody that may turn up. Mrs. Kemp will be charmed to see you."

"In that case," said Lord Thomas, "I accept with pleasure."

A pair of rough horses, in a ramshackle American wagon, were brought round, and they set forth on a ten-mile voyage through the bush, with neither lamps nor moon to steer by. At a long, swinging trot, never hastening and never loitering, the shabby animals did it in an hour without making a false step, and were as fresh at the end as at the beginning. The mysterious, illimitable gloom and the romantic solitude were very refreshing to the London man, and so was his host, who was full of merry tales and valuable information. Lord Thomas, in short, enjoyed his adventure thoroughly.

But he was taken aback by the sight of Mr. Kemp's house. Instead of the shanty of his anticipations, he beheld a tall and imposing structure, cutting a great block out of the starry midnight sky. A sweet place by daylight—ivied, virginia-creepered, grape-vined all over its mellow brick walls and decaying verandahs, with a great garden and magnificent trees around it.

"Built by my father in the early days," said Mr. Kemp. "The first big house in this district, and the only one for nigh twenty years. We've been rich folks in our time, Mr. Bone, but the ups and downs, you know—things ain't what they used to be, especially since the Boom. However, we've still got a roof over us, thank God, and a crust to share with a friend."

The family had retired, and the guest, having been warmed with whiskey, was escorted to his bedroom by the host. It was a kind of bedroom to make him feel slightly nervous about meeting the hostess next morning. The bed creaked with age, and so did the carpetless floor beneath it; but the linen was fine and the pillows soft, the handsome old rosewood furniture shone like glass, and there was an impalpable air about everything that bespoke the house of a lady.

"I don't know whether you like the windows shut?" said Mr. Kemp, hospitably bustling about.

"We always keep them open, and the blinds up. Nobody to overlook us here, you know." He tried to pull down a sash which stuck in the frame, but at Lord Thomas's request desisted.

"Leave it as it is," said the guest. "I like them open. It's so Australian!"

And he presently lay down on his lavender-perfumed couch, feeling—after his experience of bush inns—that it was the nicest bed he had ever occupied. And that scent of the earth and of the night, coming in through open windows, how exquisite it was! He blew out his candle—a homemade candle in an old chased silver candlestick—and slept like a baby.

Not for long, however. Voices called him through those open windows, and before six o'clock he was leaning out of one of them, awake and alive as he had rarely been at such an hour.

What an Arcadian world was this, in which he felt like a man new born! Air as clear as crystal, and dew shining on shrubs and trees; giant acacias and native white cedars, and pink and white oleanders that could have swallowed an ordinary bush house; the morning moon still gleaming like a jewel over the saffron sunrise and the intensely dark-blue hills. He had heard curlews in the night and frogs at the break of dawn; now the magpies were fluting all over the place, cheerful fowls were crowing, laughing jackasses shouting "Ha-ha-ha!" and "Hoo-hoo-hoo!" to one another. Delicious sounds! But none so acutely audible as the immense silence at the back of them.

"This," said he to himself, "is the real bush, that we have heard so much about, at last."

He looked down from his window, and saw the sparrows at the ripe grapes now loading the eaves of the verandah; saw a hare limping along the graveled paths, where no hare should be. He looked over the garden hedges to the peaceful fields outside, where cows were feeding quietly, throwing shadows on the wet grass; flocks of cockatoos were screaming amongst them, and sprinkling themselves like white flowers over the fresh-ploughed land; and an army of dusky jays held the vineyard on the hill, whence their joyous gabble rose continuously. It was not his property they were destroying, and he saw and heard them with delight—those denizens of the wild bush—that was healing him, body and soul, of the ills of excessive civilization.

The pink dawn spread and glowed, quenching the horned moon and dimming the sapphire hues of the distant ranges. Then some white bee boxes gleamed conspicuously to the right of the flower garden—an orderly encampment, like tents on a field of battle—and he could see the busy swarms going forth to their day's labor. He could even hear them humming, they were in such myriads. And another thing he heard—a faint, muffled clatter—which he traced

to a little building near the gate of the bees' enclosure; a shed made of reeds, with two windows and a
door in it—doubtless the honey-house, in which
some one was early at work. As he listened to the
noise within, he watched the door, which faced his
view, and presently he saw a girl come out of it. She
wore a pink cotton sunbonnet, veiled with a bushman's fly net, and an all-embracing tight apron, which
made her look like the toy figures of a Noah's ark.
In each hand she carried a long tin box, one heavier
than the other, by rough loops of fencing wire; and
she marched with them down an alley between the
beehives. Mr. Kemp had casually mentioned his
daughter, who, at the time, Lord Thomas had not
regarded as affecting him in any way. Evidently this
was she, and the circumstances of the house disposed
him to take another view of her.

He saw her put the boxes on the grass and set the
lids open, then lift the roof from one of the wooden
hives. A cloud of angry insects rose to her stooping
face and buzzed about her; it made him tingle to see
them, but she heeded them no more than if they had
been motes in the sun rays that now lighted up her
figure so effectively. She puffed something that
smoked into the open hive from a sort of little bellows arrangement, and then lifted out the frames of
comb, held them dangling in the air while she
brushed black masses of bees off them, and placed

them edgewise in one of the boxes on the grass until she had quite filled it. Out of the other she took similar frames, which she dropped into the emptied chamber, and shut down there. Then he saw her laboring towards the honey house with the weighted box, and was exasperated to note how it dragged her down. She passed it from hand to hand to ease the strain, but could not carry it without a twist of her supple body, a staggering gait, and pantings that he seemed to hear, though of course he could not.

"What a shame!" he inwardly ejaculated. And he withdrew into his room, emptied a can of water into a battered old bath, and dressed in haste. The clatter in the honey-house, which had ceased while she was amongst the bees, showing that she worked single-handed, began again.

"I wonder," quoth Lord Thomas, "what she's doing in there?"

He thought he would go down to see, and went, stepping softly, so as not to disturb the rest of the family, who did not seem to rise so early as she. As usual in the bush, no locks or bolts impeded him; he turned the handle of the hall door, and noiselessly slipped out.

What a morning indeed! Freshly autumnal—for it was the end of March—though the day would be all summer until the sun was low again; cool almost to coldness, with an air that washed the lungs and invigorated the heart in a manner to make mere living an ecstasy, even to a lord—the air of the spacious, untainted bush, and of nowhere else in the wide world. He stood a moment on the steps of the verandah to drink it in—to sniff the wholesome odor of gum trees and the richer scent of the perennial orange flower starring the thick green walls of the orchard paths. Then he strolled down one of those perfumed lanes—the one that divided the back garden from the front—and presented himself at the gate of the bee enclosure just as Miss Kemp, with one of her tin boxes, dashed out of the honey-house and slammed the door behind her, disappointing the expectations of a cloud of besieging bees.

She saw him and stopped short, evidently taken aback, and conscious of her coarse apron and limp sunbonnet, not worn for company. He hesitated for a moment in sympathetic confusion, but, being immediately aware that the form thus plainly outlined was a charming one, as also the pink face in the frame of pink calico, stood his ground and modestly accosted her. He lifted his cap gracefully, and a bee got under it.

"Good morning—you brute!" was what he said.

"Don't come," she cried in answer, waving him back. Then she pulled off a sticky glove and held a bare hand over the gate, regardless of bees, expressing a polite astonishment at his being up so soon.

"I heard of your arrival, Mr. Bone," said she. "I hope you slept well. I hope you like Australia, as far as you have seen it."

They chatted conventionally for some minutes. He apologized for his presence, and she reassured him, on behalf of the family, with an easy frankness that seemed to say he was but one of dozens of Mr. Bones flowing in a continuous stream through the house, like tramps through a casual ward. And then he begged to be allowed to help her in her work. "I am sure," said he, "you must want somebody to carry that heavy box—oh, conf—! They knew I am a stranger, evidently."

"Go away," she laughed. "You have no business here. I don't want help—I am quite used to doing it all—and you'd better go and sit on the verandah, where you can be at peace. Or wouldn't you like a stroll round? With a pipe, perhaps?"

"Will you show me round?"

"I'm sorry I can't; I must be busy here. The honey is coming in so fast this weather—which may break at any moment—that I can't gather it quickly enough. I get on an average nearly a quarter of a ton per day."

She looked at him with an air of professional pride, forgetting her costume; and he looked at her. The closer view showed freckles and a retroussé nose, without at all detracting from her charm. He could gaze full into her face without being rude, because her eyes were continually following the movements of the bees that buzzed about him. Every now and then her fingers skirmished round his head like a flight of butterflies.

Five minutes more, and she was tying a large apron round his waist, over a very old coat that did not fit him, and he was planting on his aristocratic head an aged straw hat, flounced with mosquito netting. In this costume, finished off with a pair of good gloves of his own, cheerfully sacrificed, he was allowed to pass through the gate and take up the box by its handles of fencing-wire. The sun was well above the ranges now, and every dewy leaf and blade of grass glittering.

"What a heavenly morning!" he sighed ecstatically.

"Isn't it?" she assented, and then fell to work again with an energy interesting to contemplate in a person of her sex and years. She walked between the rows of hives till she came to the one to be operated on; he walked after her, inwardly nervous, but with an air of utmost valor.

"Now be careful," said she, as she seized her little bellows. "Tuck that net into your waistcoat in front, and then lift the lid off for me."

He did as she bade him, and gasped at the spectacle presented. How all those bees managed to breathe and move, let alone work, in the space they occupied, was more than he could understand. She had no time to explain just now. While he stood rigid, and imagined bees under the hems of his trousers—for they were thick in the grass he stood on—she rapidly smoked the hive and drew out the frames of comb, heavy with honey, brushed thousands of stinging things off them, and placed them in the empty tin. From the full one she took the frames, filled only with hollow cells, which she had brought from the honey house; and these she dropped into the hive amid the masses of bees, leaving less than an inch between one wall of comb and another.

"And you make the same wax do again?" he inquired, thirsting for knowledge.

"Many times," she replied, pleased to inform his ignorance. "That comb will be refilled in about ten days. Put the lid on again, please. Gently—don't crush more than you can help. Now—"

She straightened her back and looked at him.

"Now what?" he inquired eagerly.

"Well, if you would, you might be filling the other box while I extracted."

But this was rather more than his courage was equal to. He said he was afraid he did not know enough about it yet.

"Very well; we will go and extract the lot we have."

They went to the honey-house together, and she quickly shut the door as soon as both were in. He smiled to himself as he saw her do it. The situation to him was—well, noticeable; to her it was absolutely without sentimental suggestions. The honey-house was the place for work, not for play.

It was a stuffy and a sticky place, for its little windows, as well as the door, had to be closed to keep the bees out. Ventilation depended on the loosely woven canvas lining the reed-thatched walls. Half of the floor was raised above the other half, so that the honey from the extractor, pouring from the spout upon a fine sieve, could flow downwards to the great tank, and from that into the tins which conveyed it to market. Five tons' weight of these tins were stacked on the lower floor, all filled and soldered up; and many more, Miss Kemp stated, were stored in the house.

"I used to get sixpence a pound for it," she informed him, with an anxious, business look in her pretty gray eyes; "but now the stores won't give more than threepence. It really doesn't seem worth while, at that price, taking railway charges and all, do you think it does?"

Lord Thomas did not, emphatically.

"So I am going to try exporting. I have the regulation boxes and tins—fifty-six pounds in a tin, and two tins in a case—and, as soon as I can get my hands free here, I shall prepare a consignment for the London market. I do hope that will pay! You are an Englishman, Mr. Bone—what is your opinion of the chances of a trade in Australian honey?"

With the confidence of utter ignorance, Lord Thomas assured her that there was a splendid opening. He knew people—heaps of people—who would snap it up gladly; and proposed to himself to be her purveyor to those people, comprising all the De Bohuns and his numerous lady friends.

"Oh, I am so thankful to hear you say that!" Miss Kemp ejaculated, with a heave of the chest.

"You see wool is down, and cattle selling for nothing and the value of places like this dropped to less than what they are mortgaged for; therefore something must be done. I've begun with honey, so I want to go on with it. I can increase to any extent, if I can only get a regular and paying market."

He was oddly touched, and more interested and amused than he had ever been in his life, to see a pretty girl regarding her destiny from such a point of view. It was something quite out of his experience. She really wanted to work, and not to flirt—to do something for men, instead of being done for by them. And yet there was nothing of the new woman about her. She was sweetly old-fashioned.

For instance, it gave her a visible shock to learn, in the course of miscellaneous conversation, that he had a baby ten months old and had left it behind in England.

"What!" she exclaimed tragically, "without either father or mother to look after it?"

"Oh," said he, "there are plenty of people to look after it."

"Who will—who could—like its own parents?"

"Well, you wouldn't have a fellow travel about the world with a nursery in his train—now would you?"

"I don't know how you can travel, under such circumstances."

He thought this very funny. And yet he liked it. Lady Thomas the first had detested children; Lady Thomas the second, a mother for a day, had shown no feeling for them. This girl's evident concern for his virtual orphan—who, as she said, might die of croup or convulsions without his knowing it, while he idly gadded about like an irresponsible bachelor— struck him as very interesting. She asked questions about it in an earnest way, and made him feel quite fatherly and serious. He wondered if the poor little brat was really being cared for properly, and determined to make strict inquiries by the next mail.

Conversation was not allowed to hinder business. While she talked in this friendly, human fashion, Miss Kemp worked as he had never seen a lady work before, as he had never worked himself since he was born. With a frame of comb in one hand, and in the other a big knife, kept hot in a tin of water standing on an oil-fed flame, she sheared off the capsules from the cells that had been filled and closed, leaving those that had bees in them, with the rapidity and dexterity of a performing conjuror. Then she dropped the frames into the wheel arrangement inside the extractor, and turned the handle violently—no, he turned it for her while she prepared more frames, full ones for the machine and empty ones for the tin box, and cleared up the shreds of wax, and so on. She had no regard for attitudes, nor for the state of her complexion, and it was clearly evident that she valued Lord Thomas for his services and not for himself. He had never been in such a position since he was a fag at school; in relation to a woman, never. It chagrined him a little, but pleased him much. He determined to remain Mr. Bone for the present.

Called to breakfast, he made the acquaintance of just such a hostess as he had expected—a faded woman, with a refined face and voice, English born, and homesick for her own country. He exercised upon her that art of pleasing, of which he was a master, and she was so charmed with him that she begged him to stay a little, not to run away immediately, unless bored by the dullness of the place. Her husband abetted her, with the unquestioning hospitality of the bush, which asks no more of a guest than that he shall know how to behave himself.

"And I'll show you all my improvements," said Mr. Kemp. "A good deal more than you could run through in an hour or two, or even in a day."

"Thanks, thanks," Lord Thomas murmured. "Just at present I am more interested in the honey industry than in anything else. I intend to keep bees myself when I get back, and it is a great chance for me to see all the working of the thing as it is done here. Er—er—how clear and beautiful that is!" He looked at a dish containing a square block of honey in the comb, neatly removed from the wooden frame it was made in. Letty hastened to pass it to him.

"Isn't it?" she crooned, surveying it with a maternal air. "And this is what I get only threepence for in the local market! I can't but think there must be ways of exporting it in sections, with careful packing. Don't you think if it could be brought on English breakfast tables in the comb like this there would be a great demand for it? I am sure they haven't honey to surpass our honey."

Lord Thomas was equally sure of it—convinced, indeed, that benighted England never tasted anything like it in its life. Mrs. Kemp smiled a superior British smile. Mr. Kemp pooh-poohed the fuss his daughter made over comparative trifles. What was honey, as a topic of interest for an Englishman anxious to improve his mind, compared with ensilage, and irrigation, and six-furrow ploughs?

For two precious hours Lord Thomas found himself obliged to attend to these latter subjects with what interest he could muster, and he only got away from them so soon by force of misleading insinuations to the effect that bees were his natural hobby and bee-keeping his proposed profession. At eleven o'clock he resumed his sticky apron and gloves, his old coat and his veiled old hat, with more delight than he had ever taken in clothes before—ridiculous as it seemed, even to himself—and rushed to the heated and messy honey-house as he had never rushed to a royal garden party.

Letty's hot face lighted up at sight of him. Beads of perspiration lay like dew under her clear eyes and over her pretty lips, but she cared not, neither did he. This sort of thing did not spoil the effect, as usual. "Oh, how good of you!" she exclaimed. And at once she set him to work. He buckled to with might and main, as if his life and hers depended on the amount of honey they could extract in a given time. They had two hours together, talking while they worked, growing better friends every minute.

"Saving-saving machines," said she, still harping on the one string, "are splendid, I know; but they run away with money when there isn't any money. My plan is just the opposite of father's. It mightn't be such good economy in other circumstances, but as things are it is my idea of economy. I don't know what you think."

He told her what he thought, and she told him it was beside the point. So it was. So he wanted it to be. Hard as he worked at the handle of the extractor, he worked still harder at trying to change the subject. But, though she might be led aside a step or two, she could not be wholly drawn from it.

It was worse after lunch. She said to him, with the firm air of a general directing military maneuvers, "Now you know all that is to be done in the house, so you can attend to that while I am changing the frames in the hives. Oh, never mind the box; I can carry it quite easily. And we shall get on twice as fast."

He found he had to do it—the uncapping with the hot knife, and all the rest of it—while she went back and forth outside. It was a long afternoon, and the little shed was stifling. The perspiration poured from his brow and trickled down his neck as he strained every nerve to be ready for her each time she brought the full box in. And his wages were next to nothing.

But at last the sun went down, and his long struggle to get the better of his rivals seemed over. They came straggling home in the golden twilight to their well-earned rest, and Letty Kemp prepared to follow their example when it was too dark to work any more.

"There," said she, with a sigh of utter weariness and satisfaction, "we have done well, haven't we? I can't tell you how much obliged to you I am, Mr. Bone."

Suddenly he felt tired of being Mr. Bone and a casual laborer, so he said awkwardly, "Er—er—I think you haven't got my name quite correctly. It is De Bohun—Thomas de Bohun."

"Oh, I beg pardon," she returned, in an airy manner; and he perceived that she was not enlightened. "You know, Mr. de Bohun, there is a little talk and movement about eucalyptus honey just now. Some chemist people at home have been praising its medicinal properties. And it is everything in these cases to strike while the iron is hot."

"Ye—es," drawled Lord Thomas absent-mindedly. Actually she had been so absorbed in those blessed bees as not to have heard of him in his proper character.

They took off their sticky overalls and returned to the house to prepare for the evening meal. And when Miss Kemp came downstairs, washed and brushed, in a pale-blue frock, a white muslin fichu, and a rose, Lord Thomas thought her beautiful. Yes, in spite of freckles and a turned-up nose. Never had he seen in woman's shape such pure health and such an absence of self-consciousness. Of all the charming novelties surrounding him, these were the most charming.

"I suppose she's too busy to notice what a sweet creature she is," he thought, as he sat down to the juicy slice of mutton for which he had earned so keen an appetite. And he anticipated with joy the leisure hours he now expected to spend with her, undisturbed by bees, in the somewhat threadbare drawing room.

All went thither together at the conclusion of the meal—the comfortable tea-dinner of the bush. Mr. Kemp, desiring to talk ploughs and ensilage, proposed a smoke. His guest, yearning for tobacco, aching in every limb, declined. Mrs. Kemp sent her daughter to the piano, and Letty played—admirably Lord Thomas thought—the intermezzo from *Cavalleria*, and a few things of that sort; and while he tried to listen, and to feed his sense of the girl's many-sided excellence, his hostess babbled about London as she remembered it, and wanted a thousand and one details of the dear city as it was now. During a laborious description of the Thames Embankment, Letty rose from the music-stool, and softly moved about the room. Her admirer flattered himself that she was listening to him, but was shortly undeceived. She vanished at a moment when his face was turned from the door, and never came back.

"Does she actually leave me!" he dumbly groaned. "Is she so lost to all the feelings of her sex as to imagine that I won't miss her while I have this old woman to talk to?" It was enough to drive any titled gentleman to extremities.

Soon he was hunting the dim verandahs round and round, in search of the fugitive. He explored the passages of the house; he walked about the garden, smelling so strongly of orange blossom, in the pure night air; and he used bad language under his breath.

At last he was drawn to a light shining like a thread of incandescent wire through a certain outhouse door. He lifted the latch and looked in.

There she was. Kneeling on a piece of sacking in the middle of the floor, with her blue skirt pinned up round her waist under a large apron, and with all the mess of a station workshop and lumber-shed around her, she was busily engaged in painting her brand on honey tins. A kerosene lamp shed effective rays on her dainty figure, her fair, clear skin, her shining chestnut hair. In short, Lord Thomas stood and looked at her, fascinated. Of the thousands of pretty women that he had admired in his time, not one had ever appeared to such advantage in the matter of background and grouping. Yet he protested at the sight.

"Oh, I say! Haven't you done enough work for one day, Miss Kemp? Are you trying to kill yourself?"

She looked up at him with a laugh; and her eyes, focusing the light, were like stars in the grubby gloom. "Oh, I beg your pardon, Mr. de Bohun! I thought as you were talking to mother, you would not notice if I slipped away for half an hour."

"Did you?" said Lord Thomas, entering and shutting the door behind him.

"I want so badly to get my consignment away next week. And I thought if I painted the tins to-night, they would be dry for packing in the morning."

She continued to dab her black brush upon a slip of perforated zinc, but her quick hand became slightly unsteady, and she blushed visibly, even in that bad light. The fact was that Lord Thomas—not as Lord Thomas, but as a man—was a delightful fellow, and it was not in nature that a healthy, heart-whole girl could spend a long and intimate day with him without being more or less affected in the usual way. As yet her bees were of more consequence than lovers—he was resentfully aware of it—but that did not prevent her feeling hourly more conscious that toil was sweetened by his participation therein. She was pleased that he had found her. She was more pleased when he took the black brush from her, asked leave to remove his coat, turned up his cuffs, and began to paint honey tins himself.

"I am not a very practiced hand at this sort of thing," he confessed. "You must tell me if I don't do it right."

"You are quite as practiced at that as I am at looking on while others do my work," she replied.

"So I suppose," he rejoined thoughtfully.

They had a happy hour, unmolested by the parents, who never supposed that their practical Letty could lend herself to foolishness. Lord Thomas painted all the tins successfully. He could not well go wrong while she held the lettered label straight. Their two heads were within an inch of touching as they bent over their job; a handkerchief might have covered their four hands while the branding was in process. They looked at each other's fingers continually.

"Mine," said Letty, "are quite rough compared with yours. I don't think I ever saw such beautiful nails. It's my belief you never did a stroke of work in your life until you came here."

"Well," said Lord Thomas, coloring a little, "I am afraid I haven't done much. You make me awfully ashamed of myself, Miss Kemp."

They fell into serious talk at this stage—the first serious talk Lord Thomas had ever had with a young lady, all his experiences notwithstanding.

"I wish," he abruptly remarked, "you'd teach me to be as useful as you are." There was much feeling in his voice.

She seemed to think the matter over. Then she asked him when he intended to return home. He said he was not sure.

"Soon, I suppose?"

"Oh, I suppose so."

"You must go soon," she urged. "You must, for the sake of that poor baby, left to the tender mercies of hired people."

"Well," he said, "I will."

"Then you will have an opportunity to be very, very useful. You can look after my honey for me in London—oh!"

He flung the paintbrush into the pot.

"I suppose it is useless," he exclaimed, through grinding teeth, "to expect you to care a straw for anything except honey and bees!"

There were but two courses open to a self-respecting man, titled or otherwise—to make her do it, or die in the attempt.

She is Her Grace the Duchess now. And an excellent duchess into the bargain. The smart folks laugh at her for not "knowing her way about," but the duke does not. He thoroughly realizes that she knows it better than they do. When, as a surprise present to her, he established a magnificent apiary in the castle grounds, and then found she did not care for it, he was a little disappointed; but he soon woke to the fact that bees had been merely the make-shift of circumstance until worthier objects for the exercise of her splendid abilities were provided. With great households to administer and young dukes to rear—not to speak of a thousand matters of more public moment—she advisedly transferred her interest in honey to the wives of her husband's tenants.

"But they will never make honey like mine," she says, shaking her coroneted head. "It wants the taste of the eucalyptus in it."

Love in a Garden

[HENRY CLAY LEWIS]

In the whole range of human attributes there are not two more antagonistical qualities than courage and cowardice; yet, how frequently we find them existing in the same person, ensconced under the same coat of skin! In the form that contains a spirit that would face with unblenching eye the fiercest peril of man's existence, we will often discover a timorous sprite, who hems and hesitates, and falters and trembles, at an enemy no more formidable than a pair of soft blue eyes, pouring their streams of liquid subduing tenderness, or else a brace of piercing black orbits, which, like the fire of the ancient Greeks, burn the fiercer for the water which love pours over them, in the shape of tears.

And, odd as it may seem, this discordant association of heroism and timidity is not found in weak effeminate nervous men, but in those whose almost gigantic proportions, eagle eye, and dauntless bearing convey any idea but that there is stuff for trembling in their stalwart frames. But they are the ones who generally manifest the greatest cowardice—place them before a battery of girls' eyes, and it proves literally a *galvanic* battery, shocking them to such a degree that they usually do something they never intended, and say things that they never meant. Let one of these animals be in love, and what a mess he generally makes of the affair! Did you ever know one to "pop the question" in a respectable civilized manner? That is, if he ever exalted his courage sufficiently to get that near to matrimony. My word for it—never. No suit for breach of promise could be ever brought against one of them—for such is the noncommittalism of their incoherency, that no woman, on her oath, could avow, even were they *conjugated* at the time, that he ever asked her to marry him; the intuitive feeling of her sex alone enabled her to draw the idea that he was addressing her, from the mass of his discordant, incoherent, lingual ramblings, when the question was being popped.

This philosophizing is intended as a preface or premonitory symptom of a story, illustrative of the trait; which, like measles, when repelled by cold air, has struck in upon my memory, and which, carrying out the idea, requires, like the aforesaid measles, to be brought to the surface in order that I may feel relieved.

Among the many acquaintances that my profession enabled me to make in the swamp, no one afforded me more pleasure than Jerry Wilson, the son of a small planter resident some few miles from my shingle. There was something so manly and frank in his bearing that our feelings were irresistibly attracted towards him. In my case it proved to be mutual: he seemed to take the same interest in me, and we soon became bosom friends. A severe attack of congestive fever that I carried him through successfully, riveted him to me for ever; and Jerry, upon all and every occasion, stood ready to take up the gauntlet in my defense, as willingly as in his own. Being very popular in the neighborhood, he became of great assistance to me, by advocating my cause, and extending, by his favorable representations, my circle of practice.

The plantation adjoining Jerry's father's was possessed by an old, broken-down Virginian, who, having dissipated one fortune in conforming to the requirements of fashionable life, had come into the swamp, to endure its many privations, in order that he might recruit his impoverished finances.

Adversity, or something better, had taught him the folly of the prominent foible of the Virginian—insane state pride, and consequent individual importance. His mind was prepared to test men by the proper criterion—merit, without regard to the adventitious circumstances of birth, wealth, or nativity.

Major Smith deserves the meed, I believe, for being the first one of the race to acknowledge that he was not an F. F.; which confession, showing his integrity of character, proved to me that he really was one of the very first of the land. But, in describing the father, I am neglecting by far the most interesting, if not the most important character of the story—his daughter—a sweet blooming girl of seventeen, at the time of which I write. Ah! she was the bright exemplar of her sex! Look in her eye—so luminous, yet so tender, and far down in its dreamy still waters, you could see the gems of purity and feeling glimmering; listen to her voice—and never yet forest bird, on the topmost leafy bough, gave forth such a gush of melody, as when it rose and melted away in a laugh; her modesty and timidity—you have seen the wild fawn, when, pausing on the brink of some placid lake, it sees its beautiful image reflected in the waters—thus shrank she, as if into herself, when voice of love, or praise, or admiration stole into her ears—and yet, with all her maidenly reserve and timidity, she loved and was beloved. Knowing that I am a bachelor, think not, in this recital, that my swelling heart is tearing open anew wounds which time and philosophy have just enabled me to heal. No! my fair friend—for friend she was, and is—never kindled in my heart the flames of love, or heard aught of the soft impeachment from me; for, long before I had seen her, the "Swamp Doctor" had wedded his books and calling—rather a frigid bride, but not an unprolific one, and her yearly increase, instead of bringing lines of anxiety to my brow, smoothes the wrinkles that care and deep thought— certainly it cannot be age—Lord! Lord! I have broken my wig spring—have dropped upon my visage!

My friend Jerry was the favored mortal, and, without doubt, in an equal intensity reciprocated her love; but cowardice had hitherto prevented an avowal upon his part, and the two lovers, therefore, dwelt in a delicious state of uncertainty and suspense. No one, to know Jerry, as the majority of men—going through the world with their noses either too elevated or too depressed for observation—know their kind, would have thought him a coward: but I knew, that, as respected women, a more arrant poltroon did not exist. He would have met any peril that resolution, strength, or a contempt for life could overcome, without fear of the consequences or the least tremor; and yet he dared not for his life tell a pretty girl, "that he loved her, and would be highly pleased, and sorter tickled, too, if she would marry him." There was something more terrible in the idea of such an avowal, than fighting bears, hugging Indians, or strangling panthers.

The poor girl, with the intuitive perception of her sex, had long perceived that Jerry loved her as ardently as if the avowal on his part had already been made. Almost daily she saw him, eagerly she awaited a declaration, but poor Jerry never could get his courage to the sticking point; like Bob Acres, it would ooze out at his fingers' points, in spite of himself and his determination to bring things to the condition of a fixed fact.

Matters were in this state when I became fully acquainted with them; she was willing, he was willing, and yet, if they kept on in the way they were pursuing, they both bid fair to remain in single blessedness for a long time to come. Deeply interested in the welfare of both parties, I thought I could not manifest my sympathy better than by kindly intervening and producing that crisis which I knew would accord with the feelings of both.

A slight attack of fever of the lady's, not requiring medical aid, but which a father's fears magnified, and would not be allayed until I had been sent for, introduced me fully to the confidence of the daughter; and a trite experiment, which I tried upon her, convinced me that all that my friend Jerry had to do was to ask, and it would be given.

Holding my fair patient's hand, which, resting in mine, looked like a pearl in a setting of jet, I placed my fingers upon her pulse, and, whilst pretending to number it, accidentally, as it were, mentioned Jerry's name—the sudden thrill that pervaded the artery assured me that she loved—lifting my eyes to her face, I gave her an expressive look, which suffused her beauteous countenance, as if she was passing into the second stage of scarlet fever.

My next duty was to seek Jerry. I found him seated on a log, under a shady willow by the edge of the bayou, pole in hand, assuming to be angling. The tense state of his line, and an occasional quiver of the pole, indicated that a fish was hooked. Passing unnoticed by him, a stranger would have come to one of three conclusions: that he was deranged, in love, or a born fool.

Walking up to him briskly, without his hearing me, although I made considerable noise getting down the bank, I slapped him on the shoulder to engage his attention, and, as I had several patients to visit, and time was precious, without waiting for the usual salutations of the day, commenced my address in a real quarter race manner:

"Jerry, for a sensible man, and a fellow of courage, you are the d——dest fool and coward unhung. You love a girl—the girl loves you. You know that the old people are willing, and that the girl is only waiting for you to pop the question, to say 'Yes!' and yet, instead of having the thing over. . . and becoming the head of a respectable family, here you sit, like a knot on a tree, with the moss commencing to grow on your back, pretending to be fishing, and yet not knowing that a big cat is almost breaking your line to shivers.

"Now I want to do you a service, and you must take my advice. Jerk that fish out, take the hook out of his mouth, and then put him back in the bayou—perhaps his sweetheart was waiting for him when he got hung; and as you are in a like predicament, you should be able to say to the gal, 'That mercy I to others show, that mercy show to me!' Go home, put on a clean shirt, shave that hair off your face and upper lip; for a sensible woman never yet accepted a man, with nothing but the tip of his nose visible from its wilderness of hair. Dress yourself decently, go up to old Smith's, wait till you get rested, then ask the girl to take a walk in the garden—gardens are a hell of a place to make love in—to look at the flowers, to eat radishes, to pluck grapes—anything for an excuse to get her there—and when you have got her under the arbor, don't fall on your knees, or any of your fool novel notions, but stand straight up before her, take both of her hands in yours, look her dead in the eyes, and ask her, in a bold, manly way—as if you were pricing pork—to marry you. Will you do it? Speak quick! I'm interested in the matter, for if you don't do it today, by the Lord, I will, for myself, tomorrow. I have held off for you long enough; and if you don't bring matters to a close, as I say, in the next twenty-four hours, as cold weather is coming on, I'll try my hand myself in the courting line—you know doctors are the very devil amongst the women!"

This method of address alarmed Jerry, and he promised he would do as I directed.

Accompanying him home, I saw him fairly dressed, and then left him, as the demands of my patients were urgent.

Jerry mounted his steed, and set off at a brisk canter for Major Smith's. It was only a mile and a half, and would have been traveled in a quarter of an hour, had the steed kept his gait. But, somehow, as the distance shortened, the canter ceased, and a pace superseded it; the last half, his rate had moderated to a walk; and when he made the last turn in the road, his horse was browsing the grass and cane. Up to the last few hundred yards, Jerry was as brave as a panther with cubs, and determined on following out my prescription to the letter; but the moment the house, with its white chimneys, commenced appearing round the bend of the bayou, the white pin feathers began to peep out in his heart, and verily, nothing, I believe, but my threat, if he proved recreant today, of courting her myself on the morrow, kept him from giving up the chase, and retracing his steps home.

But the house was reached, and the hearty voice of the Major, bidding him alight, cut off all retreat. He was fairly in it.

Jerry got down, left the yard gate carefully open behind him, led his horse up the Major's fine grass-walk to the steps, and was about bringing him with him into the house, when a servant relieved him of the task by carrying the steed to the stable. Not noticing the air of astonishment with which the old Major was regarding him, he shook hands with the Negro for Major Smith, and bowing to a large yellow water-jar, addressed it as "Miss Mary," and then finished the performances by sitting down in a large basket of eggs; the sudden yielding of his seat, and the laughter of both father and daughter, aroused him to a full consciousness of how ridiculously he was acting. His apologies and explanations only served to render bad worse, and he therefore wisely determined to take a chair and say nothing more. Dinner was shortly announced, and this he concluded in very respectable style, without making any more serious mistake than eating cabbage with a spoon, or helping the lady to the drumstick of the chicken. A cigar was smoked after dinner, and then the old Major, giving a shrewd guess how the land lay, declared that he must take his afternoon nap, and retired, leaving the field to Jerry and the daughter. "Now or never," was the motto with Jerry.

The old Major, in addition to planting cotton, and retrieving a dissipated fortune, was a great dabbler in horticulture, and had bestowed great attention upon the cultivation of the grape. By much care and grafting, he had so improved upon the common varieties of the country as to render them but slightly inferior to the choicest foreign specimens. An extensive arbor was in the middle of the garden—the finest and most extensive in the swamp—and this was literally covered with the ruddy clusters of grapes, now in the fullest tide of ripeness.

"Now or never," I say, was the word with Jerry. Making a desperate effort, he faltered out, "Miss Mary, your father has a very fine garden! shall we go look at the grapes? I am very fond of them, Miss Mary! do you like grapes, Miss Mary? Ha! ha!"—the cold sweat bursting out from every pore.

"Very much, Mr. Wilson, and Pa's are really very fine, considering that they have not the quality of being exotics to recommend them to our taste. I will accompany you to taste them with much pleasure," replied Miss Mary; and tripping into the house, soon appeared, with the sweetest little sunbonnet on, that witching damsel ever wore.

Jerry, frightened nearly to death at the awful propinquity of the "question popping," could scarcely stand, for his agitation; and poor Miss Mary, apprehending from Jerry's manner that the garden was destined to become the recipient of some awfully horrible avowal—perhaps Jerry had murdered somebody, and his conscience was forcing him to disclose. . . or—surely he was not going to make a declaration—oh, no! she knew it was not anything of that kind—began to participate in Jerry's embarrassment and trepidation. More like criminals proceeding to execution, than young people going to pluck grapes, they sought the garden; the gate was closed behind them, and in a few moments more they stood under the arbor.

The grapes were hanging down upon all sides in the greatest profusion; and, twining their purple masses together, seemingly cried out, "Come eat us!"

Jerry was the very picture of terror. Oh! how he wished that he was safe at home! But it was too late to retreat—he could only procrastinate. But still, men had gone as far as walking in a secluded garden with a lady, and then died old bachelors. But then that infernal doctor tomorrow—the die was cast, he would go on. The question was, how should he approach the subject, so as not to destroy life in the young lady, when the dreadful business of his visit was announced? He must prepare her for it gradually—the grapes offered an introductory—the impolite fellow, not to offer her any during the long time they had been in the arbor—they had just a second before reached it.

Plucking off a large bunch, he handed them to her, and selected a similar one for himself. They were devoured in silence, Jerry too badly frightened to speak, and Mary wondering what in the world was to come next. The grapes were consumed, another pair of bunches selected, and the sound of their champing jaws was all that broke the stillness. Jerry's eyes were fixed on his bunch, and Mary was watching the motions of an agile snail. The cluster was in process of disappearance, when Jerry, summoning his whole energies, commenced his declamation: "Miss Mary, I have something to impart"—here he came to a full stop, and looked up, as if to draw inspiration from heaven; but the umbrageous foliage intercepted his view, and only the grapes met his eye—and their juice requires to be gone through with several processes, before much exhilaration or eloquence can be drawn from it. Plucking a quantity, he swallowed them, to relieve his throat, which was becoming strangely dry and harsh.

Miss Mary, poor girl, was sitting there, very much confused, busily eating grapes; neither she nor Jerry knew, whilst continuing to eat, the quantity that they had consumed: their thoughts were elsewhere.

"Miss Mary," again upspoke Jerry, "you must have seen long before this—but la! your bunch is eaten—have some more grapes, Miss Mary? I like them very much"—and amidst much snubbling and champing, another package of grapes was ware-housed by the lovers.

Jerry's fix was becoming desperate; time was flying rapidly, and he knew one subject would soon be exhausted, for he could eat but few more grapes. Oh! how he wished that fighting a panther, fist-fight, had been made one of the conventialities of society, and assumed to be declaratory of the soft passion! how quickly would his bride be wooed!—but those infernal words! he could never arrange them so as to express what he meant. "Miss Mary, you must know that I saw Dr. Tensas, today, he told me—have some more, Miss Mary, they won't hurt you. I have come expressly to ask you—have another bunch, let me insist. I have come, Miss Mary, to pro-pose—another small bunch"—"Mary, I have come," he almost shrieked, "to ask you to have—only a few more—Oh! Lord!" and he wiped the cold sweat off. Poor fellow! his pluck would not hold out.

Mary, frightened at his vehemence, said nothing, but ate on mechanically, anxious to hear what it was that Jerry wished to disclose.

Again he marshaled his forces: the sun was declin-ing in the west, and the morrow would, perhaps, see the "Swamp Doctor," with his glib tongue, breath-ing his vows—"Miss Mary, I—I love—grapes—no, you—grapes—will you have me—some grapes—marry me—no grapes—yes, me! Oh! Lord! it is all over! You will—bless you—I must have a kiss. You haven't consented yet—but you must!" The barrier seemed to drop, the spell was lifted off his tongue, and Jerry, in a stream of native eloquence, running the fiercer for being so long pent up plead his cause; could it be unsuccessful? Oh! no! Mary had made up her mind long ago.

Side by side, now, all their diffidence vanished; they sat under the blessed arbor, and discoursed of their past fears, and bright hopes for the future! Jerry held the head of his mistress on his leal and noble breast, and, as in a sweet and pure strain he pictured forth the quiet domestic life they were to lead when married, Mary could scarcely believe that the impudent fellow who now talked so glibly, and stole, in spite of her rebukes, kisses unnumbered, was the timid nervous swain of a few minutes before.

But lo! behold what a sudden transformation! Has Jerry struck some discordant note in his sweet melody of the future—for Mary's features are contracted, as if with pain, and her pretty face, in spite of herself, wears a vinegar aspect. Rather early, I opine, for ladies to commence the shrew—if I am wrong, lady reader, attribute the error to the ignorance of an old bachelor. Jerry, too, seems to partake of the sour contagion—he stamps upon the ground, writhes his body about, and presses his hand upon his stomach, ignorant, I presume, of anatomy. He meant to lay them over his heart, poor fellow! he got too low down. Mary, too, is evincing the ardency of her affection; and with the same deplorable ignorance of the locality of the organs. Verily, love is affecting them singularly. It may be a pleasant passion, but that couple, who certainly have a fresh, I will not say genuine, article of love, look like anything but happy accepted lovers. What can be the matter? They have just read an extract from one of Cowper's bucolics— but can poetry produce such an effect? They groan, and writhe their bodies about, and would press their hearts, if *they* only lay where their digestive apparatus certainly does. Can the grapes have anything to do with their queer contortions?

"Heavens!" Jerry cries, as a horrid suspicion flashes over his mind, "The cholera! The cholera! Dearest, we will die together, locked in each other's arms!" and Jerry sought to embrace his lady love; but she was scrunched up, I believe the ladies term it, and as he had assumed the same globular position, approximation could not be effected, and death had acquired another pang, from their having to meet him separate.

Fortunately for them, the Major had got his sleep out some hours before, and, becoming anxious at their prolonged stay, set out to seek them. As the garden was a quiet, secluded place, he thought them most likely to be there, and there he found them, laboring under the influence, not so much of love as—the truth must out—an overdose of grapes: and you know how they affect the system.

A boy was dispatched post haste after me. Fortunately I was at home, and quickly reached the spot. I reached the house, and was introduced immediately to the apartment where both the patients lay. A glance at their condition and position explained the cause fully of their disease. A hearty emetic effected a cure; and the first child of Jerry and Mary Wilson was distinctly marked on the left shoulder with a bunch of grapes.

What She Wore

[EDNA FERBER]

Somewhere in your story you must pause to describe your heroine's costume. It is a ticklish task. The average reader likes his heroine well dressed. He is not satisfied with knowing that she looked like a tall, fair lily. He wants to be told that her gown was of green crepe, with lace ruffles that swirled at her feet. Writers used to go so far as to name the dressmaker; and it was a poor kind of a heroine who didn't wear a red velvet by Worth. But that has been largely abandoned in these days of commissions. Still, when the heroine goes out on the terrace to spoon after dinner (a quaint old English custom for the origin of which see any novel by the "Duchess," page 179) the average reader wants to know what sort of a filmy wrap she snatches up on the way out. He demands a description, with as many illustrations as the publisher will stand for, of what she wore from the bedroom to the street, with full stops for the ribbons on her robe de nuit, and the buckles on her ballroom slippers. Half the poor creatures one sees flattening their noses against the shop windows are authors getting a line on the advance fashions. Suppose a careless writer were to dress his heroine in a full-plaited skirt only to find, when his story is published four months later, that full-plaited skirts have been relegated to the dim past!

I started to read a story once. It was a good one. There was in it not a single allusion to brandy-and-soda, or divorce, or the stock market. The dialogue crackled. The hero talked like a live man. It was a shipboard story, and the heroine was charming so long as she wore her heavy ulster. But along toward evening she blossomed forth in a yellow gown, with a scarlet poinsettia at her throat. I quit her cold. Nobody ever wore a scarlet poinsettia; or if they did, they couldn't wear it on a yellow gown. Or if they did wear it with a yellow gown, they didn't wear it at the throat. Scarlet poinsettias aren't worn, anyhow. To this day I don't know whether the heroine married the hero or jumped overboard.

You see, one can't be too careful about clothing one's heroine.

I hesitate to describe Sophy Epstein's dress. You won't like it. In the first place, it was cut too low, front and back, for a shoe clerk in a downtown loft. It was a black dress, near-princess in style, very tight as to fit, very short as to skirt, very sleazy as to material. It showed all the delicate curves of Sophy's underfed, girlish body, and Sophy didn't care a bit. Its most objectionable feature was at the throat. Collarless gowns were in vogue. Sophy's daring shears had gone a snip or two farther. They had cut a startlingly generous V. To say that the dress was elbow-sleeved is superfluous. I have said that Sophy clerked in a downtown loft.

Sophy sold "sample" shoes at two-fifty a pair, and from where you were standing you thought they looked just like the shoes that were sold in the regular shops for six. When Sophy sat on one of the low benches at the feet of some customer, tugging away at a refractory shoe for a would-be small foot, her shameless little gown exposed more than it should have. But few of Sophy's customers were shocked. They were mainly chorus girls and ladies of doubtful complexion in search of cheap and ultra footgear, and—to use a health term—hardened by exposure.

Have I told you how pretty she was? She was so pretty that you immediately forgave her the indecency of her pitiful little gown. She was pretty in a daringly demure fashion, like a wicked little Puritan, or a poverty-stricken Cleo de Merode, with her smooth brown hair parted in the middle, drawn severely down over her ears, framing the lovely oval of her face and ending in a simple coil at the neck. Some serpent's wisdom had told Sophy to eschew puffs. But I think her prettiness could have triumphed even over those.

If Sophy's boss had been any other sort of man he would have informed Sophy, sternly, that black princess effects, cut low, were not *au fait* in the shoe-clerk world. But Sophy's boss had a rhombic nose, and no instep, and the tail of his name had been amputated. He didn't care how Sophy wore her dresses so long as she sold shoes.

Once the boss had kissed Sophy—not on the mouth, but just where her shabby gown formed its charming but immodest V. Sophy had slapped him, of course. But the slap had not set the thing right in her mind. She could not forget it. It had made her uncomfortable in much the same way as we are wildly ill at ease when we dream of walking naked in a crowded street. At odd moments during the day Sophy had found herself rubbing the spot furiously with her unlovely handkerchief, and shivering a little. She had never told the other girls about that kiss.

So—there you have Sophy and her costume. You may take her or leave her. I purposely placed these defects in costuming right at the beginning of the story, so that there should be no false pretenses. One more detail. About Sophy's throat was a slender, near-gold chain from which was suspended a cheap and glittering La Valliere. Sophy had not intended it as a sop to the conventions. It was an offering on the shrine of Fashion, and represented many lunch-less days.

At eleven o'clock one August morning, Louie came to Chicago from Oskaloosa, Iowa. There was no hay in his hair. The comic papers have long insisted that the country boy, on his first visit to the city, is known by his greased boots and his high-water pants. Don't you believe them. The small-town boy is as fastidious about the height of his heels and the stripe of his shift and the roll of his hat-brim as are his city brothers. He peruses the slangily worded ads of the "classy clothes" tailors, and when scarlet cravats are worn the small-town boy is not more than two weeks late in acquiring one that glows like a headlight.

Louie found a rooming house, shoved his suitcase under the bed, changed his collar, washed his hands in the gritty water of the washbowl, and started out to look for a job.

Louie was twenty-one. For the last four years he had been employed in the best shoe store at home, and he knew shoe leather from the factory to the ash barrel. It was almost a religion with him.

Curiosity, which plays leads in so many life dramas, led Louie to the rotunda of the tallest building. It was built on the hollow center plan, with a sheer drop from the twenty-somethingth to the main floor. Louie stationed himself in the center of the mosaic floor, took off his hat, bent backward almost double and gazed, his mouth wide open. When he brought his muscles slowly back into normal position he tried hard not to look impressed. He glanced about, sheepishly, to see if any one was laughing at him, and his eye encountered the electric-lighted glass display case of the shoe company upstairs. The case was filled with pink satin slippers and cunning velvet boots, and the newest thing in bronze street shoes. Louie took the next elevator up. The shoe display had made him feel as though some one from home had slapped him on the back.

The God of the Jobless was with him. The boss had fired two boys the day before.

"Oskaloosa!" grinned the boss, derisively. "Do they wear shoes there? What do you know about shoes, huh boy?"

Louie told him. The boss shuffled the papers on his desk, and chewed his cigar, and tried not to show his surprise. Louie, quite innocently, was teaching the boss things about the shoe business.

When Louie had finished—"Well, I try you, any-how," the boss grunted, grudgingly. "I give you so-and-so much." He named a wage that would have been ridiculous if it had not been so pathetic.

"All right, sir," answered Louie, promptly, like the boys in the Alger series. The cost of living problem had never bothered Louie in Oskaloosa.

The boss hid a pleased smile.

"Miss Epstein!" he bellowed, "step this way! Miss Epstein, kindly show this here young man so he gets a line on the stock. He is from Oskaloosa, Ioway. Look out she don't sell you a gold brick, Louie."

But Louie was not listening. He was gazing at the V in Sophy Epstein's dress with all his scandalized Oskaloosa, Iowa, eyes.

Louie was no mollycoddle. But he had been in great demand as usher at the Young Men's Sunday Evening Club service at the Congregational church, and in his town there had been no Sophy Epsteins in too-tight princess dresses, cut into a careless V. But Sophy was a city product—I was about to say pure and simple, but I will not—wise, bold, young, old, underfed, overworked, and triumphantly pretty.

"How-do!" cooed Sophy in her best baby tones. Louie's disapproving eyes jumped from the objectionable V in Sophy's dress to the lure of Sophy's face, and their expression underwent a lightning change. There was no disapproving Sophy's face, no matter how long one had dwelt in Oskaloosa.

"I won't bite you," said Sophy. "I'm never vicious on Tuesdays. We'll start here with the misses' an' children's, and work over to the other side."

Whereupon Louie was introduced into the intricacies of the sample shoe business. He kept his eyes resolutely away from the V, and learned many things. He learned how shoes that look like six dollar values may be sold for two-fifty. He looked on in wide-eyed horror while Sophy fitted a No. 5C shoe on a 6B foot and assured the wearer that it looked like a made-to-order boot. He picked up a pair of dull kid shoes and looked at them. His leather-wise eyes saw much, and I think he would have taken his hat off the hook, and his offended business principles out of the shop forever if Sophy had not completed her purchase and strolled over to him at the psychological moment.

She smiled up at him, impudently. "Well, Pink Cheeks," she said, "how do you like our little settlement by the lake, huh?"

"These shoes aren't worth two-fifty," said Louie, indignation in his voice.

"Well, sure," replied Sophy. "I know it. What do you think this is? A charity bazaar?"

"But back home——" began Louie, hotly.

"Ferget it, kid," said Sophy. "This is a big town, but it ain't got no room for back-homers. Don't sour on one job till you've got another nailed. You'll find yourself cuddling down on a park bench if you do. Say, are you honestly from Oskaloosa?"

"I certainly am," answered Louie, with pride.

"My goodness!" ejaculated Sophy. "I never believed there was no such place. Don't brag about it to the other fellows."

"What time do you go out for lunch?" asked Louie.

"What's it to you?" with the accent on the "to."

"When I want to know a thing, I generally ask," explained Louie, gently.

Sophy looked at him—a long, keen, knowing look. "You'll learn," she observed, thoughtfully.

Louie did learn. He learned so much in that first week that when Sunday came it seemed as though aeons had passed over his head. He learned that the crime of murder was as nothing compared to the crime of allowing a customer to depart shoeless; he learned that the lunch hour was invented for the purpose of making dates; that no one had ever heard of Oskaloosa, Iowa; that seven dollars a week does not leave much margin for laundry and general recklessness; that a madonna face above a V-cut gown is apt to distract one's attention from shoes; that a hundred-dollar nest egg is as effective in Chicago as a pine stick would be in propping up a stone wall; and that all the other men clerks called Sophy "sweetheart."

Some of his newly acquired knowledge brought pain, as knowledge is apt to do.

He saw that State Street was crowded with Sophys during the noon hour; girls with lovely faces under pitifully absurd hats. Girls who aped the fashions of the dazzling creatures they saw stepping from limousines. Girls who starved body and soul in order to possess a set of false curls, or a pair of black satin shoes with mother-o'-pearl buttons. Girls whose minds were bounded on the north by the nickel theatres; on the east by "I sez to him"; on the south by the gorgeous shop windows; and on the west by "He sez t' me."

Oh, I can't tell you how much Louie learned in that first week while his eyes were getting accustomed to the shifting, jostling, pushing, giggling, walking, talking throng. The city is justly famed as a hothouse of forced knowledge.

One thing Louie could not learn. He could not bring himself to accept the V in Sophy's dress. Louie's mother had been one of the old-fashioned kind who wore a blue-and-white checked gingham apron from 6 A.M. to 2 P.M., when she took it off to go downtown and help the ladies of the church at the cake sale in the empty window of the gas company's office, only to don it again when she fried the potatoes for supper. Among other things she had taught Louie to wipe his feet before coming in, to respect and help women, and to change his socks often.

After a month of Chicago Louie forgot the first lesson; had more difficulty than I can tell you in reverencing a woman who only said, "Aw, don't get fresh now!" when the other men put their arms about her; and adhered to the third only after a struggle, in which he had to do a small private washing in his own wash-bowl in the evening.

Sophy called him a stiff. His gravely courteous treatment of her made her vaguely uncomfortable. She was past mistress in the art of parrying insults and banter, but she had no reply ready for Louie's boyish air of deference. It angered her for some unreasonable woman-reason. There came a day when the V-cut dress brought them to open battle. I think Sophy had appeared that morning minus the chain and La Valliere. Frail and cheap as it was, it had been the only barrier that separated Sophy from frank shamelessness. Louie's outraged sense of propriety asserted itself.

"Sophy," he stammered, during a quiet half-hour, "I'll call for you and take you to the nickel show tonight if you'll promise not to wear that dress. What makes you wear that kind of a getup, anyway?"

"Dress?" queried Sophy, looking down at the shiny front breadth of her frock. "Why? Don't you like it?"

"Like it! No!" blurted Louie.

"Don't yuh, rully! Deah me! Deah me! If I'd only knew that this morning. As a gen'ral thing I wear white duck complete down t' work, but I'm savin' my last two clean suits f'r gawlf."

Louie ran an uncomfortable finger around the edge of his collar, but he stood his ground. "It—it—shows your—neck so," he objected, miserably.

Sophy opened her great eyes wide. "Well, supposin' it does?" she inquired, coolly. "It's a perfectly good neck, ain't it?"

Louie, his face very red, took the plunge. "I don't know. I guess so. But, Sophy, it—looks so—so—you know what I mean. I hate to see the way the fellows rubber at you. Why don't you wear those plain shirtwaist things, with high collars, like my mother wears back home?"

Sophy's teeth came together with a click. She laughed a short cruel little laugh. "Say, Pink Cheeks, did yuh ever do a washin' from seven to twelve, after you got home from work in the evenin'? It's great! 'Specially when you're living in a six-by-ten room with all the modern inconveniences, includin' no water except on the third floor down. Simple! Say, a child could work it. All you got to do, when you get home so tired your back teeth ache, is to haul your water, an' soak your clothes, an' then rub 'em till your hands peel, and rinse 'em, an' boil 'em, and blue 'em, an' starch 'em. See? Just like that. Nothin' to it, kid. Nothin' to it."

Louie had been twisting his fingers nervously. Now his hands shut themselves into fists. He looked straight into Sophy's angry eyes.

"I do know what it is," he said, quite simply. "There's been a lot written and said about women's struggle with clothes. I wonder why they've never said anything about the way a man has to fight to keep up the thing they call appearances. God knows it's pathetic enough to think of a girl like you bending over a tubful of clothes. But when a man has to do it, it's a tragedy."

"That's so," agreed Sophy. "When a girl gets shabby, and her clothes begin t' look tacky she can take a gore or so out of her skirt where it's the most wore, and catch it in at the bottom, and call it a hobble. An' when her waist gets too soiled she can cover up the front of it with a jabot, an' if her face is pretty enough she can carry it off that way. But when a man is seedy, he's seedy. He can't sew no ruffles on his pants."

"I ran short last week," continued Louie. "That is, shorter than usual. I hadn't the fifty cents to give to the woman. You ought to see her! A little, gray-faced thing, with wisps of hair, and no chest to speak of, and one of those mashed-looking black hats. Nobody could have the nerve to ask her to wait for her money. So I did my own washing. I haven't learned to wear soiled clothes yet. I laughed fit to bust while I was doing it. But—I'll bet my mother dreamed of me that night. The way they do, you know, when something's gone wrong."

Sophy, perched on the third rung of the sliding ladder, was gazing at him. Her lips were parted slightly, and her cheeks were very pink. On her face was a new, strange look, as of something half forgotten. It was as though the spirit of Sophy-as-she-might-have-been were inhabiting her soul for a brief moment. At Louie's next words the look was gone.

"Can't you sew something—a lace yoke—or whatever you call 'em—in that dress?" he persisted.

"Aw, fade!" jeered Sophy. "When a girl's only got one dress it's got to have some tong to it. Maybe this gown would cause a wave of indignation in Oskaloosa, Iowa, but it don't even make a ripple on State Street. It takes more than an aggravated Dutch neck to make a fellow look at a girl these days. In a town like this a girl's got to make a showin' some way. I'm my own stage manager. They look at my dress first, an' grin. See? An' then they look at my face. I'm like the girl in the story. Muh face is muh fortune. It's earned me many a square meal; an' lemme tell you, Pink Cheeks, eatin' square meals is one of my favorite pastimes."

"Say looka here!" bellowed the boss, wrathfully. "Just cut out this here Romeo and Juliet act, will you! That there ladder ain't for no balcony scene, understand. Here you, Louie, you shinny up there and get down a pair of them brown satin pumps, small size."

Sophy continued to wear the black dress. The V-cut neck seemed more flaunting than ever.

It was two weeks later that Louie came in from lunch, his face radiant. He was fifteen minutes late, but he listened to the boss's ravings with a smile.

"You grin like somebody handed you a ten-case note," commented Sophy, with a woman's curiosity. "I guess you must of met some rube from home when you was out t' lunch."

"Better than that! Who do you think I bumped right into in the elevator going down?"

"Well, Brothah Bones," mimicked Sophy, "who did you meet in the elevator going down?"

"I met a man named Ames. He used to travel for a big Boston shoe house, and he made our town every few months. We got to be good friends. I took him home for Sunday dinner once, and he said it was the best dinner he'd had in months. You know how tired those traveling men get of hotel grub."

"Cut out the description and get down to action," snapped Sophy.

"Well, he knew me right away. And he made me go out to lunch with him. A real lunch, starting with soup. Gee! It went big. He asked me what I was doing. I told him I was working here, and he opened his eyes, and then he laughed and said: 'How did you get into that joint?' Then he took me down to a swell little shoe shop on State Street, and it turned out that he owns it. He introduced me all around, and I'm going there to work next week. And wages! Why say, it's almost a salary. A fellow can hold his head up in a place like that."

"When you leavin'?" asked Sophy, slowly.

"Monday. Gee! it seems a year away."

Sophy was late Saturday morning. When she came in, hurriedly, her cheeks were scarlet and her eyes glowed. She took off her hat and coat and fell to straightening boxes and putting out stock without looking up. She took no part in the talk and jest that was going on among the other clerks. One of the men, in search of the missing mate to the shoe in his hand, came over to her, greeting her carelessly. Then he stared.

"Well, what do you know about this!" he called out to the others, and laughed coarsely, "Look, stop, listen! Little Sophy Bright Eyes here has pulled down the shades."

Louie turned quickly. The immodest V of Sophy's gown was filled with a black lace yoke that came up to the very lobes of her little pink ears. She had got some scraps of lace from—Where do they get those bits of rusty black? From some basement bargain counter, perhaps, raked over during the lunch hour. There were nine pieces in the front, and seven in the back. She had sat up half the night putting them together so that when completed they looked like one, if you didn't come too close. There is a certain strain of Indian patience and ingenuity in women that no man has ever been able to understand.

Louie looked up and saw. His eyes met Sophy's. In his there crept a certain exultant gleam, as of one who had fought for something great and won. Sophy saw the look. The shy questioning in her eyes was replaced by a spark of defiance. She tossed her head, and turned to the man who had called attention to her costume.

"Who's loony now?" she jeered. "I always put in a yoke when it gets along toward fall. My lungs is delicate. And anyway, I see by the papers yesterday that collarless gowns is slightly passay f'r winter."

Love and Lightning

[**JOHN OAKUM**]

C.	Gregory Jones had been courting a girl by wire for about three years, and had corresponded with her by mail until an engagement of marriage had been finally settled between them, "sight unseen," it being inconvenient for them to meet, on account of the distance, she being located some four hundred miles away from him.

> *What could be expected when we note*
> *their common labors,*
> *What when we consider that the two*
> *had long been neighbors,*
> *Not so near that they had met, but*
> *near enough—'Tis true,*
> *Little distances may lend enchantment*
> *to a view.*

In the same office with Jones there worked a stylish youth by the name of John Birdsong, and so partial was the fair telegrapher to Jones that whenever he went to dinner, and she was compelled to work the wire with Birdsong, they invariably quarreled about something or other, and became, in the course of time, as cordial enemies as she and Jones were friends. Birdsong lost no opportunity to wound her feelings, and she often told him that if she ever laid eyes on him she would tell him to his face what she thought of him in such terse and vigorous English as to leave no doubt in his mind about the position he occupied in her estimation. Thus matters stood, when one day Jones attired himself in gorgeous plumage to go and see his own true love, and left on the evening train. He arrived in due time, and they were mutually pleased with each other. I will not stop to dwell on the subject of their billing and cooing— there was no end to it, it is safe to assume. But his furlough ran along like the wind, and all too soon came the sad hour of parting. He was to return by the midnight train, and they had long since closed the little office at the depot and adjourned to the old farm house—her father's residence—in the suburbs of the village. It was a beautiful moonlight night in the early September, and the scene out of doors upon which they had long been gazing, talking of their happiness and the prospect of quick coming nuptials, meantime, had wrought them up to the sublimest pitch of ecstatic bliss. You nor I, reader dear, will never know the half they said that night; no, indeed. As the last hour of Jones's stay was wearing on, the joy of his soul arose and lighted a lamp. She then went and brought from an adjoining room his natty light overcoat and glossy beaver. She sat the latter on the table while she assisted him on with his coat her hands leaning lovingly on his shoulders, and, then, while he was settling himself into his coat she went and took up the hat and stood looking into it, waiting to pass it to him. Her sweet face flushed, her eyes downcast, she looked almost heavenly in his eyes, and he said: "Ah! darling, you are more beautiful than Phyrne, and —"

At that moment the hat sped across the room and she fell to attacking her lover in the choicest epithets of abuse that ever fell from a pretty woman's lips. He tried to soothe her, but she would not answer any questions, and Jones hearing his train whistle, and knowing he must positively return home that night, went and picked up the shako and ran mournfully to the depot, and she sat weeping as if her heart would break in the old room which had witnessed so many scenes of love and devotion between them. Probably no man was ever more wretched than Jones as the night express rumbled out of the quiet village and sped onward. But he was a philosophic young man, withal, so he went into the smoking car, lighted a cigar, and began to think the matter over. The more he thought about it, the more he was puzzled. He pictured her standing there, pretty and patient, holding his hat, and suddenly he said to himself: "I wonder if there is anything about that *hat* which disturbed the girl?" and he took it off and looked at it. It had a great dent on the side of it, to be sure, but that wasn't there when she had it. Then he looked inside and he grew pale, for there in capital letters appeared the unhappy name—John Birdsong. It all came to him then; he had borrowed Birdsong's new fall tile, at the last moment, to make his *tout ensemble* altogether irresistible, and he knew very well, Birdsong had often told her, when she and he had indulged in a difference, that if she didn't behave better he would come down some day, tell her he was Jones, and let her say "pretty things" to him.

I will not weary you with the details of the explanations which followed, or the conciliation afterward. Ours is an age in which people clamor for results, not means, so let me conclude by stating that Birdsong helped to bring the matter to a happy settlement, and finally stood up with Jones at the wedding in the same old parlor where his hat had gone scurrying from an angry hand. And if you ever pass Jones's house and see a five-year-old boy swinging on a gate, who looks like his father and speaks like the echo of his mother's voice, bear in mind that your happy eye is resting on the figure of Master John Birdsong Jones.

The Love Quarrel

[AGNES STRICKLAND]

May never was the month of love,
For May is full of flowers;
But rather April, richly kind,
For love is full of showers.
    —Father Southwell

There are partings which are truly "such sweet sorrow," that they only appear as the heralds of happier meetings; and there are partings when stern destiny imperatively divides those whom love has united so fondly, that absence but renders them the dearer to each other; and there are also partings where the inexorable hand of death severs the silver tie that has linked faithful hearts so firmly, that the extinction of life alone can loosen that tender bond of affection. Such separations are painful, but there is no bitterness in the tears which they cause—tears in which the cordial of hope, or the heavenly balm of resignation to the divine will, is gently infused, leading the mourner to look forward to a reunion with the beloved object in those happy realms where partings are unknown. But oh! how different are the feelings of those who separate in doubt, in anger, and disdain, when the wounded spirit of each is prompted, by offended pride, to veil its agonies under the semblance of coldness and indifference!

It was thus that Helen Milbourne had parted from the object of her tenderest affection, the cavalier Colonel Dagworth, in the moonlight recesses of her Uncle Ireton's garden at Irmingland Hall, where they had met, at peril of life to him and maiden fame to her. They had met in trembling hope, and with hearts overflowing with a love that neither the difference of party, rank, station, the wrath of kindred, nor the obstacles of time, absence, danger, and uncertainty, could overcome; and yet they had separated in anger, in consequence of a trifling misunderstanding that had arisen between them—a cause of offence so slight that it would have been difficult for either to have explained why it was given, or wherefore it was taken; yet it had served to rend asunder those ties of tender union which would have defied the efforts of a world combined to have unknit. They parted on

either side with a pang more bitter than the separation of soul and body, each smarting under the sense
of injurious treatment from the other, and strangely
imagining that they had mutually become, in one
short hour, the object of hatred—ay, even of scorn—
to the being most fondly beloved on earth. And oh,
if pride would have permitted either to allow their
natural emotions of tenderness and grief to be per-
ceptible to the other, how different would have been
the result of their first—their last—their only quarrel!
As it was, Colonel Dagworth, agitated and distressed
by the painful conviction of the hopeless position of
the royal cause, and the ruin that impended over
himself in common with all who nobly adhered to
the fallen fortunes of his unhappy sovereign, deigned
not to offer the slightest attempt at apology or conciliation to the wealthy heiress of the Parliamentary
Commissioner, Ralph Milbourne, and the niece of
the victorious Roundhead chieftain, Ireton; but,
loosening the bridle-rein of his gallant gray from the
withered arm of one of the stunted sallows that over-
hung the moat, he made a stern and silent parting
obeisance to her; and, vaulting into the saddle,
unconsciously vented his own intense sensation of
mental anguish, by striking the rowels of his spurs so
sharply into the sides of the faithful animal who had
patiently bided his pleasure, that the bloody streaks
on its glossy sides were distinctly visible, and would

have excited an abhorrent exclamation from Helen had she observed it. But no! she, too, in imitation of her angry lover's assumed disdain, with a haughty acknowledgment of his repulsive farewell, turned proudly away; yet it was partly to conceal the gush of tears, that overflowed her eyes at the very moment she was acting a part so foreign to her nature; and when she was sure that her motion could not be detected, she hurried to the only spot that commanded a view of the road he had taken, and eagerly strained her tearful gaze to catch a last look of his stately form, as he gained a sudden angle in the road which would conceal his further progress; and here the anxious query proposed itself to her fluttering heart: "Will he not turn his head to look once more?"

He did not. The resentful flush of wounded pride overspread the cheek of Helen, which a moment before had been of the hue of marble, and indignantly dashing away the tears that hung on its polished surface, she murmured:

"It is past!—You have spurned a true heart from you, Edward Dagworth, and I will think of you no more!"

"No more!" did Helen say? Ay, thus she said, and many a time did she repeat her words; too often, indeed to adhere to the resolution she formed in the bitterness of what she considered slighted love and wronged affection. That indignant sentence, "I will think of him no more," was the spring of all her thoughts, forbidding her to meditate on aught beside the man she was perpetually vowing she would forget. Alas! he appeared the sole tenant of her memory, so intimately was his idea entwined with every feeling of her nature. It was not in the power of either time, absence, or a sense of his injurious unkindness, to banish his loved image from her mind, though every day she repeated her vain words, "I will think of him no more!" But how could she cease to think of him, in the perilous days when the impending cloud of ruin gathered more darkly every hour over his cause, and the events of the next might lead him to a prison or a scaffold, if, indeed, he escaped the contingencies of the battlefield, or survived the hardships and dangers of the siege of Colchester, where he was now shut up with Lord Capel and the rest of its brave defenders, by the beleaguering force of Sir Thomas Fairfax.

The parents of Colonel Dagworth and Helen Milbourne had been neighbors, but not friends; they belonged to separate and distinct classes of society. The proud old Norfolk knight, Sir Reginald Dagworth, whose only son Colonel Dagworth was, looked down with unfeigned contempt on the acquired wealth and ostentatious pretensions of Master Ralph Milbourne, who had purchased large estates in his immediate vicinity; and whose magnificent new-built mansion, large establishment, and showy equipages, were calculated to excite a painful comparison with the faded splendour of his ancient family—a family that once held almost princely rank and possessions in his native country, but which, in consequence of a series of imprudences or vicissitudes, was rapidly sinking into decay.

The undesirable location of a wealthy *parvenu* neighbor was a subject of great annoyance both to Sir Reginald Dagworth and Lady Alice, his wife, who considered it incumbent on them, for the honor of their house, to make an effort to support the superiority of their claims to be the great people of the place; while Ralph Milbourne failed not on his part to testify all the offensive contempt for rank and ancestry which is one of the peculiar characteristics of vulgar pride, and on all occasions obtruded an offensive opposition to every measure Sir Reginald appeared desirous of carrying in county business. It was much to be lamented that these sylvan foes had nothing better to occupy their time and thoughts than a hostile *espionage* on each other's actions, and an eager and unworthy attention to the exaggerated reports of servants and dependents of what each said of the other; for by this means a feud so deadly was fostered, that the breaking out of the civil war between the king and parliament was privately hailed by both with a degree of satisfaction, as affording an excuse for those open acts of violence and aggression which the laws had hitherto operated to prevent. They were arrayed, of course, on opposite sides, for Sir Reginald Dagworth was a part of the old *régime*—a concomitant ingredient of that system which it was the object of the republican party to destroy; and Ralph Milbourne's hatred of that privileged class, which, he was sensible, looked down on him and his golden claims to consideration with contempt, was such, that he was willing to hazard even the loss of that wealth which he secretly worshipped, to assist in humbling its haughty and hated members. There were but two things he loved on earth—his money and his one fair daughter; whom he regarded as its heiress, and prized her perhaps more dearly on that account than for all the charms both of mind and person with which nature had so richly endowed her.

But though he professed such hostility of feeling against the whole order of aristocracy, which was then, as at the present moment, peculiarly denounced by a party as the authors of all the existing or fancied evils in the state, he was secretly desirous of his descendants in the third generation being members of this vituperated body, through the marriage of his daughter with no less a person than the heir of his sworn enemy; and deeply mortified at the apparent insensibility of young Dagworth to the attractions of his lovely daughter, and his blindness to the pecuniary advantages of such an alliance, he was perpetually venting his chagrin by contemptuous expressions respecting him; constantly warning Helen never to degrade herself by bestowing a thought upon him; protesting that, if she condescended to be made a convenience of, by wedding the heir of impoverished greatness, to patch up the fallen fortunes of his house with her wealth, he would utterly renounce her.

These cautions were, perhaps, in the first instance, the occasion of making Edward Dagworth an object of attention to his fair neighbor; for she concluded that he must have given her father some reason for an observation so otherwise unaccountable to her. She even ventured to imagine that overtures of a matrimonial nature must have been indirectly, if not directly, made; and she felt a sort of trembling anxiety to ascertain how far the heart of Edward Dagworth had been interested in the proposition.

It was then that she first became aware of the majestic beauty of his features, and the air of lofty rectitude and amiable frankness which they expressed; and then, he was so different from the stern sectarians, rude levelers, and wily politicians, whom she was accustomed to meet at the house of her Uncle Ireton! With neither of these classes had she a feeling or sympathy in common; their manners were offensive to her taste, and she regarded their projects for the subversion of the laws and religion of her forefathers with alarm and terror; while the dread that she might one day be made the bond and victim of a conventional plight between the men of her family and some influential party leader, perpetually haunted and disquieted her. In contradistinction to a destiny so revolting to her feelings, she was at times tempted to picture to her youthful fancy the possibility of becoming the wife of Edward Dagworth, till the idea became a fondly cherished hope; and she even felt pleasure in the thought of devoting her wealth to the very purpose so earnestly contemned by her father, that of building up the ruined fortunes of his ancient house; of which every member, even those haughty parents of his, who regarded her and hers as beings far beneath their high *caste*, became objects of powerful interest to her.

Edward Dagworth meantime was far from being unconscious of the charms of his lovely neighbor; and in such cases there is always a sort of undefined intelligence which silently informs a pair so situated as these were, that they are becoming dear to each other. It is certain that the eyes of both met oftener than they were accustomed to do; and on meeting were mutually withdrawn in confusion, till at length, without having exchanged a single sentence of love, they were reciprocally wooed and won, and mutely established on the footing of lovers.

Their parents, their friends, the world suspected it not; but they understood each other's feelings, and that was enough for them. Opportunity alone was needed to cement those silent vows of love and lasting faith before the altar of God.

The erection of the royal standard at Nottingham, and the eventful scenes that followed, served to remove them from their dreaming bliss. The storm of civil war had burst upon the land, and was arraying brothers against brothers, fathers against sons; no wonder, then, if rivals and political foes were espousing adverse causes.

Edward Dagworth engaged in the service of his insulted sovereign with no common ardor; and his name was soon proudly distinguished among the gallant partisans of the royal cause. Even the hoary-headed knight, his father, forgot the infirmities of age to assume the cuirass and steel cap, and sentenced the last of his oak groves to the axe, to assist in raising a regiment for the service of the king.

Ralph Milbourne, though little qualified to play the soldier, found himself a person of consequence with the adherents of the parliament, to whom his wealth was, in the outset of their enterprise, before they had obtained the power of making the cavaliers pay the charges of the warfare against themselves, a matter of great importance; and for the use of this they were contented not only to allow him the exorbitant interest he demanded, but bestowed upon him, in addition, both civil and military rank in their embryo republic; paying him, at the same time, those flattering compliments and attentions that had always been the objects of his ambition, and the lack of which, the mainspring of his disaffection to the government and of his hatred to the higher classes. Neither his wealth, his magnificent establishment, nor his assumption of consequence, had been able to procure for him, in the neighborhood of his Norfolk estates, the respect he coveted. Sir Reginald Dagworth was evidently regarded there as a sort of hereditary sovereign by the peasantry and yeomanry; and the profound homage with which every member of this ancient but impoverished family was treated, was the generous, unbought offering of the heart, which gold could never purchase.

Ralph Milbourne was evidently considered as an upstart stranger, and the more he added house to house, and field to field, the greater object of dislike did he become in that neighborhood; where loyalty was esteemed as a virtue, and enmity to the church was regarded as a crime. For a time, Ralph Milbourne quitted Norfolk for a residence in the metropolis, which his pecuniary transactions with the leaders of his party rendered necessary. London was in the hands of the Roundheads. A splendid mansion in Aldermanbury, the sequestered property of a cavalier nobleman, was bestowed upon him by the parliament; and Helen Milbourne, far removed from any chance or hope of seeing the only man for whom she had ever entertained the slightest affection, was placed at the head of a magnificent establishment, and compelled to play the courteous hostess, as mistress of her father's house, to men who were bent on the overthrow of everything which her natural sense of right, and above all, her love for Edward Dagworth, taught her to hold dear—men, too, who mentioned the name of that distinguished partisan of loyalty, as he was now considered, with hostility, who panted for his blood, and had vowed his death either in the field or on the scaffold.

And from some of these she was compelled to listen to solicitations of marriage backed by paternal authority; and though she had hitherto been permitted to put a decided negative on all their pretensions, yet, with reason, she apprehended a time would come when she would be denied the privilege of refusing some abhorrent candidate for her hand. Her cheek lost its bloom, and her eye its brightness. Her father observed the change, and became anxious on account of her health.

"I want to breathe the fresh air and enjoy the quiet retirement of the country," she replied to his inquiry.

Her father took her to a seat purchased for the occasion in one of the beautiful villages near London;

where he visited her every day, bringing home with him such of his political friends as he was desirous of uniting in still stronger bonds of fellowship with himself and family. This species of society was as distasteful to Helen as the London residence; and though her father employed every art and luxury that taste and ingenuity could suggest or wealth procure to adorn her new abode, his daughter still appeared listless and dissatisfied with all his arrangements; and when he asked her if she did not like it, she replied:

"It is not Norfolk, and it is thither I wish to go— to our own house, where I was so free and happy."

"You are a foolish girl," her father rejoined, and left her in displeasure.

The next time he came to see her he brought one of the most eminent physicians of the day to visit her; who, as soon as he had conversed with the invalid, prescribed the very thing she required— Norfolk air.

Ralph Milbourne was out of humor. It was very inconvenient to him to leave London; but Helen was his only child, and had been, of course, a spoiled child hitherto, invariably accustomed to the full indulgence of her will: so he agreed that she should follow it once more; and, much against his own inclination, conducted her to his Norfolk residence.

The very sight of the place put him into a fit of the spleen. It had not been inhabited for four years, and the country people had testified their affection to Sir Reginald Dagworth, and their dislike to him, by demolishing his windows and dilapidating his ornamental buildings in his absence. The garden had become a wilderness; his park had almost degenerated into commonage; his fences and enclosures were all broken down; and, in short, everything bore evidence of the evil odor in which his memory had been held.

Even Helen felt uncomfortable at the aspect of the place, though she endeavored to conceal the impression it created.

At that unhappy period of disorganization and anarchy, it was no easy matter to procure efficient workmen to repair the damage that had been committed. Ralph Milbourne was precise and particular in all his habits; and since his reentrance into public life he had acquired a taste for luxury and ease quite at variance with the state of his Norfolk mansion. He reproached his daughter for having been the means of bringing him to such a scene of discomfort—reviled his steward for having permitted his property to suffer such injury—execrated the Dagworths as the cause of it—and scolded his servants for their awkward attempts at repairing the mischief. As for Helen, she was patient and resigned; for she could see the gray towers of Dagworth Castle from the broken casements of her bedchamber, and she anticipated the possibility of beholding their future lord at some moment which she trusted was not remote.

After a week of angry excitement on the part of Mr. Commissioner Milbourne, of outward submission but inward resentment secretly treasured up against a day of retribution, on that of his dependents, and of quiescent endurance on that of his daughter, Ingworth New Hall, as his residence was called, was put into a habitable state; and effectual measures taken for repairing the gratuitous injuries that had been perpetrated in the grounds, gardens, and enclosures. Helen was not long in ascertaining that Sir Reginald Dagworth and his son were both absent from the neighborhood, and Lady Alice and her servants were the only residents at the Castle—intelligence as satisfactory to her father as it was the reverse to her; for persisting in attributing all the damage his property had sustained to the enmity of the old cavalier and his son, he said, "He could now safely return to London, since the Dagworths were absent, who were the only persons likely to molest his daughter in his absence."

The country appeared tolerably quiet; proper precautions had been taken to increase the securities of the house, and four resolute, well-armed male servants were deemed by Ralph Milbourne sufficient guard for his daughter during his temporary absence from her.

For two days after his departure everything remained in a state of tranquility; but on the third night Helen was roused from feverish slumbers by the savage yells of the clubmen, a rustic but fierce banditti, composed for the most part of the unemployed population of the agricultural counties throughout England, who, deprived of regular work and wages by the ruin of many of their former masters, and the distracted state of the times, had been at length driven to the desperate expedient of obtaining a predatory livelihood by collecting in formidable bands for the purpose of levying contributions on passengers, plundering the unguarded villages or solitary mansions, and, in short, of committing every sort of outrage which opportunity might offer. To these were joined men who were inimical to both the great contending parties; reckless profligates, whose crimes had rendered them the outcasts of society; and ruined spend-thrifts and unprincipled ruffians, whose tempers would not brook the restraints of anything in the shape of law or discipline.

The clubmen of that district, amounting to several hundred men, were headed by one of the latter class, who had conceived the daring project of besetting the house, and of carrying off the only daughter of the rich Parliamentary Commissioner Milbourne, for the sake of extorting a large sum of money for her ransom.

The plan was successful: the mansion was surprised and entered by the rude outlaws; and scarcely had the terrified Helen time to rise and wrap herself in a large cloak, which she hastily threw over her night-dress, when the sanctuary of her chamber was invaded by a heterogeneous band of desperadoes; the foremost of whom, with a coarse expression of admiration, seized her in his profane arms, and forcibly hurried her, in spite of her shrieks, entreaties, and resistance, into a covered carriage, which they had provided for the purpose of the abduction.

A single glance, even in the terror and confusion of that fearful moment, had been sufficient to convince Helen that they were not cavaliers into whose power she had fallen; and the Roundheads would not, of course, have attacked the house of one of their own party. She then recalled to her remembrance many passages in the diurnals, where mention had been made of the clubmen, and of the outrages perpetrated by them. With an impulse of horror which no language can describe, at the idea of the probable fate that awaited her, she called on Edward Dagworth to save her, forgetting how many miles in all probability divided them; yet, strange to say, her cry was heard and answered by him whose name she had almost deliriously invoked.

He had been ordered by his commander on a secret service in that very neighborhood, which, having successfully performed, he was on his way to join the army again, when he received intelligence of the intention of the clubmen to surprise the house of Ralph Milbourne, and carry off his daughter. He had therefore ambushed himself and his brave followers in a copse on the confines of the park, and Helen's agonizing cry for help was his signal for attacking the ruffians.

The night was profoundly dark; but the red blaze from the New Hall, which the lawless miscreants, after plundering it, had fired, was sufficient to enable the cavaliers to discharge their petronels with deadly effect among the foremost of the clubmen, who were greatly superior in numbers to themselves; then rushing from their concealment with drawn swords, they assailed them so fiercely that the rabble-rout were panic-stricken, and after a disorderly attempt at maintaining their ground, fled precipitately in all directions.

Helen, on whose startled ear the discharge of firearms, the clash of swords, and the mingled yells of rage and vengeance had fallen in dread confusion, added a faint cry of female terror to the tumultuous din around her, and sank back in a state of utter insensibility. How long her swoon continued Helen knew not; but her first sensation of consciousness was a feeling that her peril was over, for she was supported in the arms and on the bosom of some person whose form was indistinct in the surrounding darkness, but whose voice of deep and tender melody, as he gently soothed her with assurances that she was safe, and all danger past, though it had never before met her ear, went to her heart like the remembered tones of some dear familiar friend.

"And where am I?" she asked.

"With friends, madam," was the reply of her unknown protector.

"What friends?" she eagerly demanded, as a sudden volume of flame from the burning mansion threw a fitful radiance over the waving plumes and lovelocks of the cavaliers.

"With Colonel Dagworth and a part of his regiment," replied he on whose bosom she had hitherto so confidingly leaned.

"Colonel Dagworth!" she exclaimed. "Edward Dagworth, the son of Sir Reginald Dagworth, my father's enemy," continued she, gently struggling to disengage herself from his supporting arms; "is it indeed, to your generous valor that I am indebted for deliverance from a fate too terrible to think upon?"

She shuddered, and gave way to a convulsive burst of hysterical weeping; then raising her streaming eyes to his face, she murmured, "How shall we ever repay you?"

"I am repaid," he soothingly replied; "richly, nobly repaid, by the happiness I feel in having had it in my power to perform a service for Mistress Helen Milbourne."

What sweet words were these from the lips of the hero of her mental romance! Insensibly her eyes closed once more; and she was again supported on the manly bosom of her brave deliverer.

Meantime, Ingworth New Hall was blazing bright and far; a brisk wind was abroad, and, truth to tell, no efforts had been made for its preservation from the devouring element; so that, before Helen was sufficiently composed to give directions whither she should be removed, Colonel Dagworth had taken the resolution of conveying her to his own home, and placing her under his mother's protection.

Lady Alice received her fair charge with evident reluctance, but with all the outward courtesy and attention to her comforts that the circumstances of the case and the obligatory duties of hospitality required; but there was a haughtiness in her condescension that sufficiently indicated how much it cost her to exercise it towards the individual thus thrown upon her charity. Colonel Dagworth saw and felt it all more deeply than even the apprehensive and sensitive Helen; and being well aware, from his knowledge of his mother's peculiar disposition, that remonstrances from him would be perfectly useless, he endeavored to compensate to Helen, whom he regarded as his own guest, by every graceful and delicate attention, for the coldness of her reluctant hostess. Insensibly his anxious solicitude for her comforts assumed a more tender and decided character; the incipient spark of youthful passion that had long lain dormant in his bosom was once more kindled, and finally fanned into active existence by the more intimate knowledge, which personal intercourse afforded him, of the amiable qualities and intellectual endowments of her whose external charms had first captivated his youthful fancy. As for Helen, she was in a state of dreaming bliss, from which she dreaded every moment to be rudely awakened by a summons from her father. The coldness and *hauteur* of Lady Alice she regarded not; or if she did, she felt that its endurance was but a trifling counterbalance for the delight of being near him she loved, and of finding herself the object of his attentions, the cynosure of his ardent gaze.

Lady Alice was *his* mother, and she felt that from *his* mother she could have endured anything, and for her, she could have stooped to perform the most menial offices, without an idea of thereby incurring degradation. She studied her looks, she watched to anticipate her slightest wishes, and paid her the respectful homage of a dutiful and affectionate child.

Edward Dagworth possessed a mind to appreciate and understand the motives of Helen Milbourne for conduct so gratifying to himself; and too manly, too devoted in his love to trifle with the feelings of a heart like hers, he took an early opportunity of declaring himself to her; and Helen, the happy Helen, shamed not to acknowledge in return that he was, and ever had been, the object of her tenderest affections. The only obstacle to this unusual smooth course of true love was the apprehension that its consummation in the holy bands of wedlock would be opposed by their respective parents; and Helen assured him that the consent of his would and must be an indispensable preliminary to their union.

Edward Dagworth was an only and fondly beloved child, and flattered himself with the hope that his hitherto unbounded influence with his mother might overcome her reluctance to his connecting himself with the daughter of one so distasteful to their principles as the Parliamentary Commissioner Milbourne. He erred in this supposition: Lady Alice's suppressed indignation at his undisguised attentions to her fair guest found bitter vent when he ventured to hint at the nature of his feelings towards her; and, after a torrent of angry and scornful invectives, she told him that when he had procured the consent of the old Roundhead usurer Milbourne, and the blessing of his own loyal and nobly descended father, to such a union, then she would permit him to name the subject again to her.

"Agreed, madam," replied her son; and in the self-same hour, after exchanging a tender farewell with Helen, he commenced his journey to the headquarters of the royal army at Reading, where his father was; having previously despatched a letter by a trusty messenger to Ralph Milbourne, informing him of the safety of his daughter, and the state of their mutual sentiments.

The anxiety of Ralph Milbourne had reached its climax respecting the fate of his only, his beloved child, before this communication reached him; and had he learned that Helen was the wedded wife of the most impoverished gentleman in the royal army, his paternal feelings would have taught him to consider it a blessed alternative to the horrible fate of having become the victim of ruffians so abhorrent to both parties as the leaders of the clubmen.

All angry and bitter enmities towards the Dagworths appeared converted into sentiments of grateful acknowledgment and respect, when, two days after the receipt of Colonel Dagworth's letter, he presented himself at their Castle gate, to tender in person his consent to the marriage of his heiress with her pre-server; which, advantageous as it now was in every worldly sense, he concluded was no less desired by the parents of the lover than by himself. As for the state of his daughter's feelings on the subject, a look, a single glance at her animated countenance and rapture-beaming eyes as she sprang to his arms, when he entered the drawing-room of Lady Alice Dagworth, was sufficient to convince him that his consent alone was required to make her the happiest of women. Her late peril had roused all the love of a fond parent in his heart, and, folding her lovely glowing form to his bosom, he whispered, "Fear nothing; you shall be the wife of your brave preserver, Helen."

Helen could not speak, but she wept her thanks on her father's neck; then, suddenly recollecting where she was, she wiped away the mingled tears that hung upon her fair cheek, and timidly presented the Parliamentary Commissioner to Lady Alice, as her father.

Lady Alice coldly and distantly acknowledged the profound obeisance of the disconcerted Milbourne; who was advancing with eager alacrity to salute her ladyship, when a single glance from her large majestic eyes had the effect of paralyzing his motions, and silencing the compliments he was preparing to utter.

At that moment—that critical moment, and before the ungracious words which hung on the haughty lips of Lady Alice could be pronounced, the rapid sound of a horseman, riding as if on life and death, was heard crossing the drawbridge of the Castle; and the next moment, Colonel Dagworth, with the red stains of recent battle on his array, and mired from spur to plume, rushed into the apartment.

"Mother!—sweet Helen!" he exclaimed, "I have been successful—joy with me—I am the happiest of men!"

"What now?" replied Lady Alice, haughtily rising from her seat; "what mean these stains upon your dress, Colonel Dagworth—are you wounded?"

"Nothing but a scratch not worth the caring for," he replied, "the loss of the precious minutes was all my uneasiness; and for the first time in my life I would rather not have done battle with the Round-heads, had I not been intercepted by an ambuscade of them about five miles off. I should have been with you three hours earlier, but they compelled me to tarry by the way till I had beaten them soundly, mother mine; and now, I am come to tell you the good news of that, and the still better intelligence, that I have obtained my father's full and free consent to take this lady to wife."

"Your father's consent!" echoed Lady Alice; "impossible! he would never so far forget himself."

"It is here under his own hand and seal, never-theless," replied Colonel Dagworth, presenting his mother with a paper.

She received it with a compressed brow, read it with evident displeasure, and when she had con-cluded it, rent it into a thousand pieces, and scorn-fully setting her foot on the fragments, passionately exclaimed:

"Thus do I trample on the record of Sir Reginald Dagworth's weakness, and the base preliminary for an alliance with the blood of traitors—"

"And on the happiness of your only son, madam," retorted Colonel Dagworth bitterly, concluding the sentence; "of him whom you *say* you love, but the deadliest offices of hatred are kindness in comparison to the deliberate cruelty of conduct like yours."

"Helen," said the mortified parent to his daughter, who stood like one stunned and paralyzed by this unexpected ebullition of Lady Alice's hostile feelings, "it is enough; I thought the sacrifice had been on our part, when I consented to bestow you and the uncounted thousands to which you are the sole heiress, on the penniless son of an impoverished family, and an adherent to a ruined cause withal; but you have been rejected, my girl, with contumely, which ought to teach you the folly of desiring such unequal yoking; and now, Helen, return your thanks to this proud lady for the ungracious benefits she has conferred upon you, and let us begone from these walls for ever."

"Stay, Master Milbourne, for pity's sake—Helen, will you thus abandon me?" exclaimed Colonel Dagworth. "My mother," added he, "must and shall apologize for her conduct; it is the warmth of party feeling, nothing else, believe me, and you must forgive her."

"Lady Alice is your mother, Edward Dagworth," said Helen, "and from her I can forgive anything— even her assurance that I am unworthy of the honor of becoming your wife."

She curtsied with respectful dignity to both mother and son as she concluded, and, turning on the beloved of her heart the glance of tender farewell she could not trust her quivering lips to speak, passively yielded to the impulse of the paternal arm that led her from their mansion.

The recent conflagration at New Hall having left Ralph Milbourne without a Norfolk residence, and Helen still expressing a wish to remain in that county, he placed her with her Uncle Ireton's family, then occupying a spacious but dismal mansion in that neighborhood, called Irmingland Hall. And there, in spite of danger and the precautions of her family to prevent these meetings, did the adventurous lover seek, and ofttimes succeed in obtaining, stolen interviews with his beloved; and in the last of these, that rupture took place between them which I have recorded in the commencement of my tale, and which left them both angry, but broken-hearted.

The fierce excitement of the perilous and active scenes in which he was engaged, and the increasing darkness that now overshadowed his cause, seemed at times to divert the thoughts of Colonel Dagworth from the regrets and sorrows of a love that nothing could obliterate; but Helen, in the deep retirement and unbroken gloom of Irmingland Hall, had no other employment for her thoughts than heart-corroding recollections of past happiness and wronged affection. From the haughty daughter of Cromwell, who had recently become the wife of her Uncle Ireton, she neither expected nor obtained sympathy for that oppressive anguish which preyed upon the springs of life. To this time brought no balm, but rather added a twofold cause of distress—in the danger that threatened the still dear but estranged and distant object of her faithful affection; and in the uneasiness she endured in consequence of the solicitations of marriage which she now received from Sir Richard Warden, one of the Parliamentary leaders, and the chosen friend of her Uncle Ireton, by whom his cause was warmly espoused. It was also earnestly backed by her father; and could she have forgotten Colonel Dagworth, it is possible she might have yielded to the pressing instances of those near relatives in favor of one to whom she could not deny her esteem, and who possessed everything to recommend him to the regard of any one who had affections to bestow.

The fall of Colchester at length took place, and the besiegers, enraged at the obstinacy of its brave defenders, had long vowed a signal vengeance against the most distinguished of these, among whom Colonel Dagworth might be justly reckoned. His father had fallen in one of the desperate sorties that had been attempted by the cavaliers; and to all the other causes of animosity existing against this brave loyalist, was the circumstance of his being the beloved of the wealthy heiress of Ralph Milbourne, the suspected obstacle that prevented her marriage with a powerful Roundhead partisan. His death was therefore resolved upon, both as a matter of public and private expediency, by the council assembled at Colchester, soon after the surrender of that last stronghold of loyalty.

Helen Milbourne had scarcely recovered from the horror with which the ungenerous massacre of Sir John Lisle and Sir Charles Lucas had inspired her, when Lady Alice Dagworth, attired in her weeds of recent widowhood, rushed into the apartment where, with pale cheeks and tearful eyes, she had just perused the diurnal which detailed the last scene of those ill-fated heroes, and flinging her arms wildly about her, exclaimed, with a frantic shriek, "Save my son!"

"Your son!" echoed Helen, looking fearfully upon Lady Alice, and scarcely appearing to comprehend the nature of the very peril which she had so much dreaded.

"Yes, yes, my son, my only one, Edward Dagworth! The barbarous traitors who have slain Lucas and Lisle have vowed his death—the death of my beautiful, my valiant son! You loved him once, Helen Milbourne, and you can save him, if you will."

Helen Milbourne, forgetful of past injury, insult, and scorn, clung to the bosom of Lady Alice with the fervent embrace of a child; and, mingling her tears with those with which the agonized mother was bedewing her features, sobbed out:

"Alas! Lady Alice, how can I save Colonel Dagworth—I who am so powerless?"

"You are not powerless—you are the daughter of Ralph Milbourne, the niece of Ireton. Through these men you can do everything. Oh, Helen, Helen! do not waste the precious moments in vain words, but remember the fate from which he saved you, and plead for him with those who will else be his murderers!"

Helen scarcely breathed till she found herself in the presence of her uncle, who was in deep consultation with her father and Sir Richard Warden, and, flinging herself at the feet of Ireton, she preferred her suit with hysterical sobs.—He listened to her in stern silence.—She turned to her father with clasped hands and streaming eyes, and exclaimed:

"Will you not speak, my father, one word, one little word, to preserve his life who rescued your child from a fate more dreadful than death?"

"It would be useless, Helen," he replied; "he is not my prisoner—it rests with your uncle Ireton."

"He is the captive of my bow and spear!" exclaimed Ireton. "I hold his death-warrant in my hand, which is directed to me for execution, but—you can ransom him, if you will." He glanced significantly at Sir Richard Warden, who stood, with folded arms, gazing intently upon the weeping supplicant. Helen shuddered, and looked imploringly at her father.

"There is no other alternative," observed Ralph Milbourne.

"None?" said Helen, turning to Ireton.

"None," he replied, "but your consenting to become the wife of the brave Sir Richard Warden; on which condition I will allow your hand to cancel the death-warrant of the malignant Edward Dagworth."

He held it towards her as he spoke. One glance upon that fatal instrument was sufficient to decide the wavering purpose of Helen Milbourne.

"He *shall* live!" she said, tearing the warrant as she spoke; "he will not be more lost to me than he is now, when I am the wife of another; and I—I—I shall have saved him. But," added she, turning once more to her uncle, "you must engage for his liberty as well."

"I will be your uncle's surety for that, madam," said Sir Richard Warden.

"And I must see him once more."

"To what purpose?" said her father.

She covered her face, and burst into a flood of tears.

Her affianced bridegroom took her cold hand, and led her to an apartment barred and guarded, at the door of which, on the bare floor, with disheveled hair, was seated Lady Alice Dagworth in her sable garments. She started from her recumbent posture, and, grasping Helen's arm with a convulsive pressure, gasped out, "My son! my son!"

"I have saved him," said Helen, in a broken voice.

"May the God of mercy bless and reward you, then," murmured Lady Alice, snatching her to her bosom with a wild burst of weeping.

At a sign from Sir Richard Warden, the bolts were withdrawn, and Helen Milbourne and her lost lover looked upon each other once more. His noble form was war-worn and attenuated by famine. Her cheek was faded by the canker-worm of sorrow, the luster of her eyes had been dimmed by tears, and were still red and swollen from excessive weeping; in the impress of that unutterable woe which appeared imprinted on her agonized brow, Edward Dagworth read, as he supposed, his death doom. Coldness, anger, and pride were alike forgotten in each; and, fondly extending his fettered arms towards her, he exclaimed:

"And have you then come, my beloved, like an angel visitant, to my dreary prison-house, to bless me with one last look?'

"To look my last upon you, I am indeed come," she replied, "my Edward! Mine! do I say? Ay, mine; for I have purchased you with a price. You were, an hour ago, reckoned with the dead, but now are you living and free. Your life and liberty are my gift—go, and be happy; and when the green grass waves over the early grave of Dame Helen Warden (as I must soon be called), remember she died to save you from the fate of your brave companions in arms, Lisle and Lucas."

"And will you, dare you, wed this lady on such terms?" demanded Colonel Dagworth, turning sternly to Sir Richard Warden.

"No," he replied, "I'll none of her; take her—she is yours. I will bestow her upon you with my own hand at the marriage altar; and all I ask in return is, for you to bear me witness among your brother cavaliers, that you found one generous foe among the conquerors of Colchester."

Mrs. Knollys

[FREDERIC JESUP STIMSON]

I

Mrs. Knollys was a young English bride, sunny-haired, hopeful-eyed, with lips that parted to make you love them—parted before they smiled, and all the soft regions of her face broke into attendant dimples. And then, lest you should think it meant for you, she looked quickly up to "Charles," as she would then call him even to strangers, and Charles looked down to her. Charles was a short foot taller, with much the same hair and eyes, thick flossy whiskers, broad shoulders, and a bass voice. This was in the days before political economy cut Hymen's wings. Charles, like Mary, had little money, but great hopes; and he was clerk in a government office, with a friendly impression of everybody and much trust in himself. And old Harry Colquhoun, his chief, had given them six weeks to go to Switzerland and be happy in, all in celebration of Charles Knollys's majority and marriage to his young wife. So they had both forgotten heaven for the nonce, having a passable substitute; but the powers divine overlooked them pleasantly and forgave it. And even the phlegmatic driver of their *Einspänner* looked back from the corner of his eye at the *schöne Engländerin*, and compared her mentally with the far-famed beauty of the Konigssee. So they rattled on in their curious conveyance, with the pole in the middle and the one horse out on one side, and still found more beauty in each other's eyes than in the world about them. Although Charles was only one-and-twenty, Mary Knollys was barely eighteen, and to her he seemed godlike in his age, as in all other things. Her life had been as simple as it had been short. She remembered being a little girl, and then the next thing that occurred was Charles Knollys, and positively the next thing she remembered of importance was being Mrs. Charles Knollys; so that old Mrs. Knollys, her guardian aunt and his, had first called her a love of a baby, and then but a baby in love. All this, of course, was five-and-forty years ago, for you know how old she was when she went again to Switzerland last summer—three-and-sixty.

They first saw the great mountains from the summit of the Schafberg. This is a little height, three-cornered, between three lakes; a natural Belvedere for Central Europe. Mr. and Mrs. Knollys were seated on a couch of Alpine roses behind a rhododendron bush watching the sunset; but as Charles was desirous of kissing Mrs. Knollys, and the rhododendron bush was not thick enough, they were waiting for the sun to go down. He was very slow in doing this, and by way of consolation Knollys was keeping his wife's hand hidden in the folds of her dress. Undoubtedly a modern lady would have been talking of her scenery, giving word-color pictures of the view; but I am afraid Mrs. Knollys had been looking at her husband, and talking with him of the cottage they had bought in a Surrey village, not far from Box Hill, and thinking how the little carvings and embroideries would look there which they had bought abroad. And, indeed, Mrs. Charles secretly thought Box Hill an eminence far preferable to the Venediger, and Charles's face an infinitely more interesting sight than any lake, however expressive. But the sun, looking askance at them through the lower mist, was not jealous; all the same he spread his glory lavishly for them, and the bright little mirror of a lake twinkled cannily upward from below. Finally it grew dark; then there was less talking. It was full night when they went in, she leaning on his arm and looking up; and the moonbeam on the snowy shoulder of the Glockner, twenty leagues away, came over, straightway, from the mountain to her face. Three days later, Charles Knollys, crossing with her the lower portion of the Pasterzen glacier, slipped into a crevasse, and vanished utterly from the earth.

II

All this you know. And I was also told more of the young girl, bride and widow at eighteen; how she sought to throw herself into the clear blue gulf; how she refused to leave Heiligenblut; how she would sit, tearless, by the rim of the crevasse, day after day, and gaze into its profundity. A guide or man was always with her at these times, for it was still feared she would follow her young husband to the depths of that still sea. Her aunt went over from England to her; the summer waxed; autumn storms set in; but no power could win her from the place whence Charles had gone.

If there was a time worse for her than that first moment, it was when they told her that his body never could be found. They did not dare to tell her this for many days, but busied themselves with idle cranes and ladders, and made futile pretences with ropes. Some of the big, simple-hearted guides even descended into the chasm, absenting themselves for an hour or so, to give her an idea that something was being done. Poor Mrs. Knollys would have followed them had she been allowed, to wander through the purple galleries, calling Charles. It was well she could not; for all Kaspar could do was to lower himself a hundred yards or so, chisel out a niche, and stand in it, smoking his honest pipe to pass the time, and trying to fancy he could hear the murmur of the waters down below. Meantime Mrs. Knollys strained her eyes, peering downward from above, leaning on the rope about her waist, looking over the clear brink of the bergschrund.

It was the Herr Doctor Zimmermann who first told her the truth. Not that the good Doctor meant to do so. The Herr Doctor had had his attention turned to glaciers by some rounded stones in his garden by the Traunsee, and more particularly by the Herr Privatdocent Splüthner. Splüthner, like Uncle Toby, had his hobbyhorse, his pet conjuring words, his gods *ex machina*, which he brought upon the field in scientific emergencies; and these gods, as with Thales, were Fire and Water. Craters and flood were his accustomed scapegoats, upon whose heads were charged all things unaccountable; and the Herr Doctor, who had only one element left to choose from, and that a passive one, but knew, on general principles, that Splüthner must be wrong, got as far off as he could and took Ice. And Splüthner having pooh-poohed this, Zimmermann rode his hypothesis with redoubled zeal. He became convinced that ice was the embodiment of orthodoxy. Fixing his professional spectacles on his substantial nose, he went into Carinthia and ascended the great Venice mountains, much as he would have performed any other scientific experiment. Then he encamped on the shores of the Pasterzen glacier, and proceeded to make a study of it.

So it happened that the Doctor, taking a morning stroll over the subject of his experiment, in search of small things, which might verify his theory, met Mrs. Knollys sitting in her accustomed place. The Doctor had been much puzzled, that morning, on finding in a rock at the foot of the glacier the impression, or sign-manual as it were, of a certain fish, whose acquaintance the Doctor had previously made only in tropical seas. This fact seeming, superficially, to chime in with Splüthnerian mistakes in a most heterodox way, the Doctor's mind had for a moment been diverted from the ice; and he was wondering what the fish had been going to do in that particular gallery, and secretly doubting whether it had known its own mind, and gone thither with the full knowledge and permission of its maternal relative. Indeed, the good Doctor would probably have ascribed its presence to the malicious and personal causation of the devil, but that the one point on which he and Splüthner were agreed was the ignoring of unscientific hypotheses. The Doctor's objections to the devil were none the less strenuous for being purely scientific.

Thus ruminating, the Doctor came to the crevasse where Mrs. Knollys was sitting, and to which a little path had now been worn from the inn. There was nothing of scientific interest about the fair young English girl, and the Doctor did not notice her; but he took from his waistcoat-pocket a leaden bullet, molded by himself and marked "Johannes Carpentarius, Juvavianus, A.U.C. 2590," and dropped it, with much satisfaction, into the crevasse. Mrs. Knollys gave a little cry; the bullet was heard for some seconds tinkling against the sides of the chasm; the tinkles grew quickly fainter, but they waited in vain for the noise of the final fall. "May the Splüthner live that he may learn by it," muttered the Doctor; "I can never recover it."

Then he remembered that the experiment had been attended with a sound unaccounted for by the conformity of the bullet to the laws of gravitation; and looking up he saw Mrs. Knollys in front of him, no longer crying, but very pale. Zimmermann started, and in his confusion dropped his best brass-registering thermometer, which also rattled down the abyss.

"You say," whispered Mrs. Knollys, "that it can never be recovered!"

"Madam," spoke the Doctor, doffing his hat, "how would you recofer from a blace when the smallest approximation which I haf yet been able to make puts the depth from the surface to the bed of the gletscher at vrom sixteen hundred to sixteen hundred and sixty *meters* in distance?" Doctor Zimmermann spoke very good English; and he pushed his hat upon the back of his head, and assumed his professional attitude.

"But they all were trying—" Mrs. Knollys spoke faintly. "They said that they hoped he could be recovered." The stranger was the oldest gentleman she had seen, and Mrs. Knollys felt almost like confiding in him.

"Oh, I must have the—the body." She closed in a sob; but the Herr Doctor caught at the last word, and this suggested to him only the language of scientific experiment.

"Recofer it? If, madam," Zimmermann went on with all the satisfaction attendant on the enunciation of a scientific truth, "we take a body and drop it in the schrund of this gletscher; and the ice-stream moves so slower at its base than on the upper part, and the ice will cover it; efen if we could reach the base, which is a mile in depth. Then, see you, it is all caused by the motion of the ice—"

But at this Mrs. Knollys had given a faint cry, and her guide rushed up angrily to the old professor, who stared helplessly forward. "God will help me, sir," said she to the Doctor, and she gave the guide her arm and walked wearily away.

The professor still stared in amazement at her enthusiasm for scientific experiment and the passion with which she greeted his discoveries. Here was a person who utterly refused to be referred to the agency of ice, or even, like Splüthner, of Fire and Water; and went out of the range of allowable hypotheses to call upon a Noumenon. Now both Splüthner and Zimmermann had studied all natural agencies and made allowance for them, but for the Divine they had always hitherto proved an alibi. The Doctor could make nothing of it.

At the inn that evening he saw Mrs. Knollys with swollen eyes; and remembering the scene of the afternoon, he made inquiries about her of the innkeeper. The latter had heard the guide's account of the meeting; and as soon as Zimmermann had made plain what he had told her of the falling body, "Triple blockhead!" said he. "*Es war ihr Mann.*" The Herr Professor staggered back into his seat; and the kindly innkeeper ran upstairs to see what had happened to his poor young guest.

Mrs. Knollys had recovered from the first shock by this time, but the truth could no longer be withheld. The innkeeper could but nod his head sadly, when she told him that to recover her Charles was hopeless. All the guides said the same thing. The poor girl's husband had vanished from the world as utterly as if his body had been burned to ashes and scattered in the pathway of the winds. Charles Knollys was gone, utterly gone; no more to be met with by his girl-wife, save as spirit to spirit, soul to soul, in ultramundane place. The fair-haired young Englishman lived but in her memory, as his soul, if still existent, lived in places indeterminate, unknowable to Doctor Zimmermann and his compeers. Slowly Mrs. Knollys acquired the belief that she was never to see her Charles again. Then, at last she resolved to go—to go home. Her strength now gave way; and when her aunt left she had with her but the ghost of Mrs. Knollys—a broken figure, drooping in the carriage, veiled in black. The innkeeper and all the guides stood bareheaded, silent, about the door, as the carriage drove off, bearing the bereaved widow back to England.

III

When the Herr Doctor had heard the innkeeper's answer, he sat for some time with his hands planted on his knees, looking through his spectacles at the opposite wall. Then he lifted one hand and struck his brow impatiently. It was his way, when a chemical reaction had come out wrong.

"Triple blockhead!" said he; "triple blockhead, thou art so bad as Splüthner." No self-condemnation could have been worse to him than this. Thinking again of Mrs. Knollys, he gave one deep, gruff sob. Then he took his hat, and going out, wandered by the shore of the glacier in the night, repeating to himself the Englishwoman's words; "*They said that they hoped he could be recovered.*" Zimmermann came to the tent where he kept his instruments, and stood there, looking at the sea of ice. He went to his measuring pegs, two rods of iron: one sunk deep and frozen in the glacier, the other drilled into a rock on the shore. "Triple blockhead!" said he again, "thou art worse than Splüthner. The Splüthner said the glacier did not move; thou, thou knowest that it does." He sighted from his rods to the mountain opposite. There was a slight and all but imperceptible change of direction from the day before.

He could not bear to see the English girl again, and all the next day was absent from the inn. For a month he stopped at Heiligenblut, and busied himself with his instruments. The guides of the place greeted him coldly every day, as they started on their glacier excursions or their chamois hunting. But none the less Zimmermann returned the following summer, and worked upon his great essay in refutation of the Splüthner.

Mrs. Knollys went back to the little cottage in Surrey, and lived there. The chests and cases she brought back lay unopened in the storeroom; the little rooms of the cottage that was to be their home remained bare and unadorned, as Charles had seen them last. She could not bring herself to alter them now. What she had looked forward to do with him she had no strength to do alone. She rarely went out. There was no place where she could go to think of him. He was gone; gone from England, gone from the very surface of the earth. If he had only been buried in some quiet English churchyard, she thought—some green place lying open to the sun, where she could go and scatter flowers on his grave, where she could sit and look forward amid her tears to the time when she should lie side by side with him—they would then be separated for her short life alone. Now it seemed to her that they were far apart forever.

But late the next summer she had a letter from the place. It was from Dr. Zimmermann. There is no need here to trace the quaint German phrases, the formalism, the cold terms of science in which he made his meaning plain. It spoke of erosion; of the movement of the summer; of the action of the under-waters on the ice. And it told her, with tender sympathy oddly blended with the pride of scientific success, that he had given a year's most careful study to the place; with all his instruments of measurement he had tested the relentless glacier's flow; and it closed by assuring her that her husband might yet be found—

in five-and-forty years. In five-and-forty years—the poor Professor staked his scientific reputation on the fact—in five-and-forty years she might return, and the glacier would give up its dead.

This letter made Mrs. Knollys happier. It made her willing to live; it made her almost long to live until old age—that her Charles's body might be given back. She took heart to beautify her little home. The trifling articles she had bought with Charles were now brought out—the little curiosities and pictures he had given her on their wedding journey. She would ask how such and such a thing looked, turning her pretty head to some kind visitor, as she ranged them on the walls; and now and then she would have to lay the picture down and cry a little, silently, as she remembered where Charles had told her it would look best. Still, she sought to furnish the rooms as they had planned them in their mind; she made her surroundings, as nearly as she could, as they had pictured them together. One room she never went into; it was the room Charles had meant to have for the nursery. She had no child.

But she changed, as we all change, with the passing of the years. I first remember her as a woman middle-aged, sweet-faced, hardly like a widow, nor yet like an old maid. She was rather like a young girl in love, with her lover absent on a long journey. She lived more with the memory of her husband, she clung to him more, than if she had had a child. She never married; you would have guessed that; but, after the Professor's letter, she never quite seemed to realize that her husband was dead. Was he not coming back to her?

Never in all my knowledge of dear English women have I known a woman so much loved. In how many houses was she always the most welcome guest! How often we boys would go to her for sympathy! I know she was the confidante of all our love affairs. I cannot speak for girls; but I fancy she was much the same with them. Many of us owed our life's happiness to her. She would chide us gently in our pettiness and folly, and teach us, by her very presence and example, what thing it was that alone could keep life sweet. How well we all remember the little Surrey cottage, the little home fireside where the husband had never been! I think she grew to imagine his presence, even the presence of children: boys, curly-headed, like Charles, and sweet, blue-eyed daughters; and the fact that it was all imagining seemed but to make the place more holy. Charles still lived to her as she had believed him in the month that they were married; he lived through life with her as her young love had fancied he would be. She never thought of evil that might have occurred; of failing affection, of cares. Her happiness was in her mind alone; so all the earthly part was absent.

There were but two events in her life—that which was past and that which was to come. She had lived through his loss; now she lived on for his recovery. But, as I have said, she changed, as all things mortal change; all but the earth and the ice-stream and the stars above it. She read much, and her mind grew deep and broad, none the less gentle with it all; she was wiser in the world; she knew the depths of human hope and sorrow. You remember her only as an old lady whom we loved. Only her heart did not change—I forgot that; her heart, and the memory of that last loving smile upon his face, as he bent down to look into her eyes, before he slipped and fell. She lived on, and waited for his body, as possibly his other self—who knows?—waited for hers. As she grew older she grew taller; her eyes were quieter, her hair a little straighter, darker than of yore; her face changed, only the expression remained the same. Mary Knollys!

Human lives rarely look more than a year, or five, ahead; Mary Knollys looked five-and-forty. Many of us wait, and grow weary in waiting, for those few years alone, and for some living friend. Mary Knollys waited five-and-forty years—for the dead. Still, after that first year, she never wore all black; only silvery grays, and white with a black ribbon or two. I have said that she almost seemed to think her husband living. She would fancy his doing this and that with her; how he would joy in this good fortune, or share her sorrows—which were few, mercifully. His memory seemed to be a living thing to her, to go through life with her, hand in hand; it changed as she grew old; it altered itself to suit her changing thought; until the very memory of her memory seemed to make it sure that he had really been alive with her, really shared her happiness or sorrow, in the far-off days of her earliest widowhood. It hardly seemed that he had been gone already then—she remembered him so well. She could not think that he had never been with her in their little cottage. And now, at sixty, I know she thought of him as an old person too; sitting by their fireside, late in life, mature, deep-souled, wise with the wisdom of years, going back with her, fondly, to recall the old, old happiness of their bridal journey, when they set off for the happy honeymoon abroad, and the long life now past stretched brightly out before them both. She never spoke of this, and you children never knew it; but it was always in her mind.

There was a plain stone in the little Surrey churchyard, now gray and moss-grown with the rains of forty years, on which you remember reading: "Charles Knollys—lost in Carinthia"—This was all she would have inscribed; he was but lost; no one *knew* that he was dead. Was he not yet to be found? There was no grassy mound beside it; the earth was smooth. Not even the date was there. But Mrs. Knollys never went to read it. She waited until he should come; until that last journey, repeating the travels of their wedding days, when she should go to Germany to bring him home.

So the woman's life went on in England, and the glacier in the Alps moved on slowly; and the woman waited for it to be gone.

In the summer of 1882, the little Carinthian village of Heiligenblut was haunted by two persons. One was a young German scientist, with long hair and spectacles; the other was a tall English lady, slightly bent, with a face wherein the finger of time had deeply written tender things. Her hair was white as silver and she wore a long black veil. Their habits were strangely similar. Every morning, when the eastern light shone deepest into the ice-cavern at the base of the great Pasterzen glacier, these two would walk thither; then both would sit for an hour or two and peer into its depths. Neither knew why the other was there. The woman would go back for an hour in the late afternoon; the man, never. He knew that the morning light was necessary for his search.

The man was the famous young Zimmermann, son of his father, the old Doctor, long since dead. But the Herr Doctor had written a famous tract, when late in life, refuting all Splüthners' past, present, and to come; and had charged his son, in his dying moments, as most sacred trust, that he should repair to the base of the Pasterzen glacier in the year 1882, where he would find a leaden bullet, graven with his father's name, and the date A.U.C. 2590. All this would be vindication of his father's science. Splüthner, too, was a very old man, and Zimmermann the younger (for even he was no longer young) was fearful lest Splüthner should not live to witness his own refutation. The woman and the man never spoke to each other.

Alas, no one could have known Mrs. Knollys for the fair English girl who had been there in the young days of the century; not even the innkeeper, had he been there. But he, too, was long since dead. Mrs. Knollys was now bent and white-haired; she had forgotten, herself, how she had looked in those old days. Her life had been lived. She was now like a woman of another world; it seemed another world in which her fair hair had twined about her husband's fingers, and she and Charles had stood upon the evening mountain, and looked in one another's eyes. That was the world of her wedding days, but it seemed more like a world she had left when born on earth. And now he was coming back to her in this. Meantime the great Pasterzen glacier had moved on, marking only the centuries; the men upon its borders had seen no change; the same great waves lifted their snowy heads upon its surface; the same crevasse still was where he had fallen. At night, the moonbeams, falling, still shivered off its glassy face; its pale presence filled the night, and immortality lay brooding in its hollows.

Friends were with Mrs. Knollys, but she left them at the inn. One old guide remembered her, and asked to bear her company. He went with her in the morning, and sat a few yards from her, waiting. In the afternoon she went alone. He would not have credited you, had you told him that the glacier moved. He thought it but an Englishwoman's fancy, but he waited with her. He had never forgotten that old day. And Mrs. Knollys sat there silently, searching the clear depths of the ice, that she might find her husband.

One night she saw a ghost. The latest beam of the sun, falling on a mountain opposite, had shone back into the ice-cavern; and seemingly deep within, in the grave azure light, she fancied she saw a face turned toward her. She even thought she saw Charles's yellow hair, and the self-same smile his lips had worn when he bent down to her before he fell. It could be but a fancy. She went home, and was silent with her friends about what had happened. In the moonlight she went back, and again the next morning before dawn. She told no one of her going; but the old guide met her at the door, and walked silently behind her. She had slept, the glacier ever present in her dreams.

The sun had not yet risen when she came; and she sat a long time in the cavern, listening to the murmur of the river, flowing under the glacier at her feet. Slowly the dawn began, and again she seemed to see the shimmer of a face—such a face as one sees in the coals of a dying fire. Then the full sun came over the eastern mountain, and the guide heard a woman's cry. There before her was Charles Knollys! The face seemed hardly pale; and there was the same faint smile—a smile like her memory of it, five-and-forty years gone by. Safe in the clear ice, still, unharmed, there lay—O God! not her Charles; not the Charles of her own thought, who had lived through life with her and shared her sixty years; not the old man she had borne thither in her mind—but a boy, a boy of one-and-twenty lying asleep, a ghost from another world coming to confront her from the distant past, immortal in the immortality of the glacier. There was his quaint coat, of the fashion of half a century before; his blue eyes open; his young, clear brow; all the form of the past she had forgotten; and she his bride stood there to welcome him, with her wrinkles, her bent figure, and thin white hairs. She was living, he was dead; and she was two-and-forty years older than he.

Then at last the long-kept tears came to her, and she bent her white head in the snow. The old man came up with his pick, silently, and began working in the ice. The woman lay weeping, and the boy with his still, faint smile lay looking at them, through the clear ice-veil, from his open eyes.

I believe that the Professor found his bullet; I know not. I believe that the scientific world rang with his name and the thesis that he published on the glacier's motion, and the changeless temperature of his father's lost thermometer had shown. All this you may read. I know no more.

But I know that in the English churchyard there are now two graves, and a single stone, to Charles Knollys and Mary, his wife; and the boy of one-and-twenty sleeps there with his bride of sixty-three; his young frame with her old one, his yellow hair beside her white. And I do not know that there is not some place, not here, where they are still together, and he is twenty-one and she is still eighteen. I do not know this; but I know that all the pamphlets of the German doctor cannot tell me it is false.

Meantime the great Pasterzen glacier moves on, and the rocks with it; and the mountain flings his shadow of the planets in its face.

Romeo and Juliet

[CHARLES AND MARY LAMB]

The two chief families in Verona were the rich Capulets and the Montagues. There had been an old quarrel between these families, which was grown to such a height, and so deadly was the enmity between them, that it extended to the remotest kindred, to the followers and retainers of both sides, insomuch that a servant of the house of Montague could not meet a servant of the house of Capulet, nor a Capulet encounter with a Montague by chance, but fierce words and sometimes blood-shed ensued; and frequent were the brawls from such accidental meetings, which disturbed the happy quiet of Verona's streets.

Old lord Capulet made a great supper, to which many fair ladies and many noble guests were invited. All the admired beauties of Verona were present, and all comers were made welcome if they were not of the house of Montague. At this feast of Capulets, Rosaline, beloved of Romeo, son to the old lord Montague, was present; and though it was dangerous for a Montague to be seen in this assembly, yet Benvolio, a friend of Romeo, persuaded the young lord to go to this assembly in the disguise of a mask, that he might see his Rosaline, and seeing her compare her with some choice beauties of Verona, who (he said) would make him think his swan a crow. Romeo had small faith in Benvolio's words; nevertheless, for the love of Rosaline, he was persuaded to go. For Romeo was a sincere and passionate lover, and one that lost his sleep for love, and fled society to be alone, thinking on Rosaline, who disdained him, and never required his love, with the least show of courtesy or affection; and Benvolio wished to cure his friend of this love by showing him diversity of ladies and company. To this feast of Capulets then young Romeo with Benvolio and their friend Mercutio went masked. Old Capulet bid them welcome, and told them that ladies who had their toes unplagued with corns would dance with them. And the old man was light hearted and merry, and said that he had worn a mask when he was young, and could have told a whispering tale in a fair lady's ear. And they fell to dancing, and Romeo was suddenly struck with the exceeding beauty of a lady who danced there, who seemed to him to teach the torches to burn bright, and her beauty to show by night like a rich jewel worn by a blackamoor; beauty too rich for use, too dear for earth! like a snowy dove trooping with crows (he said), so richly did her beauty and perfections shine above the ladies her companions. While he uttered these praises, he was overheard by Tybalt, a nephew of lord Capulet, who knew him by his voice to be Romeo. And this Tybalt, being of a fiery and passionate temper, could not endure that a Montague should come under cover of a mask, to fleer and scorn (as he said) at their solemnities. And he stormed and raged exceedingly, and would have struck young Romeo dead. But his uncle, the old lord Capulet, would not suffer him to do any injury at that time, both out of respect to his guests, and because Romeo had borne himself like a gentleman, and all tongues in Verona bragged of him to be a virtuous and well-governed youth. Tybalt, forced to be patient against his will, restrained himself, but swore that this vile Montague should at another time dearly pay for his intrusion.

The dancing being done, Romeo watched the place where the lady stood; and under favor of his masking habit, which might seem to excuse in part the liberty, he presumed in the gentlest manner to take her by the hand, calling it a shrine, which if he profaned by touching it, he was a blushing pilgrim, and would kiss it for atonement.

"Good pilgrim," answered the lady, "your devotion shows by far too mannerly and too courtly: saints have hands, which pilgrims may touch, but kiss not."

"Have not saints lips, and pilgrims too?" said Romeo.

"Ay," said the lady, "lips which they must use in prayer."

"O then, my dear saint," said Romeo, "hear my prayer, and grant it, lest I despair."

In such like allusions and loving conceits they were engaged, when the lady was called away to her mother. And Romeo inquiring who her mother was, discovered that the lady whose peerless beauty he was so much struck with, was young Juliet, daughter and heir to the lord Capulet, the great enemy of the Montagues; and that he had unknowingly engaged his heart to his foe. This troubled him, but it could not dissuade him from loving. As little rest had Juliet, when she found that the gentleman that she had been talking with was Romeo and a Montague, for she had been suddenly smit with the same hasty and inconsiderate passion for Romeo, which he had conceived for her; and a prodigious birth of love it seemed to her, that she must love her enemy, and that her affections should settle there, where family considerations should induce her chiefly to hate.

It being midnight, Romeo with his companions departed; but they soon missed him, for, unable to stay away from the house where he had left his heart, he leaped the wall of an orchard which was at the back of Juliet's house. Here he had not been long, ruminating on his new love, when Juliet appeared above at a window, through which her exceeding beauty seemed to break like the light of the sun in the east; and the moon, which shone in the orchard with a faint light, appeared to Romeo as if sick and pale with grief at the superior luster of this new sun. And she, leaning her cheek upon her hand, he passionately wished himself a glove upon that hand, that he might touch her cheek. She all this while thinking herself alone, fetched a deep sigh, and exclaimed: "Ah me!"

Romeo, enraptured to hear her speak, said softly, and unheard by her: "O speak again, bright angel, for such you appear, being over my head, like a winged messenger from heaven whom mortals fall back to gaze upon."

She, unconscious of being overheard, and full of the new passion which that night's adventure had given birth to, called upon her lover by name (whom she supposed absent): "O Romeo, Romeo!" said she, "wherefore art thou Romeo? Deny thy father, and refuse thy name, for my sake; or if thou wilt not, be but my sworn love, and I no longer will be a Capulet."

Romeo, having this encouragement, would fain have spoken, but he was desirous of hearing more; and the lady continued her passionate discourse with herself (as she thought), still chiding Romeo for being Romeo and a Montague, and wishing him some other *name, or* that he would put away that hated name, and for that name which was no part of himself, he should take all herself. At this loving word Romeo could no longer refrain, but taking up the dialogue as if her words had been addressed to him personally, and not merely in fancy, he bade her call him Love, or by whatever other name she pleased, for he was no longer Romeo, if that name was displeasing to her. Juliet, alarmed to hear a man's voice in the garden, did not at first know who it was, that by favor of the night and darkness had thus stumbled upon the discovery of her secret; but when he spoke again, though her ears had not yet drunk a hundred words of that tongue's uttering, yet so nice is a lover's hearing, that she immediately knew him to be young Romeo, and she expostulated with him on the danger to which he had exposed himself by climbing the orchard walls, for if any of her kinsmen should find him there, it would be death to him, being a Montague.

"Alack," said Romeo, "there is more peril in your eye, than in twenty of their swords. Do you but look kind upon me, lady, and I am proof against their enmity. Better my life should be ended by their hate, than that hated life should be prolonged, to live without your love."

"How came you into this place," said Juliet, "and by whose direction?"

"Love directed me," answered Romeo: "I am no pilot, yet wert thou as far apart from me, as that vast shore which is washed with the farthest sea, I should venture for such merchandise."

A crimson blush came over Juliet's face, yet unseen by Romeo by reason of the night, when she reflected upon the discovery which she had made, yet not meaning to make it, of her love to Romeo. She would fain have recalled her words, but that was impossible: fain would she have stood upon form, and have kept her lover at a distance, as the custom of discreet ladies is, to frown and be perverse, and give their suitors harsh denials at first; to stand off, and affect a coyness or indifference, where they most love, that their lovers may not think them too lightly or too easily won; for the difficulty of attainment increases the value of the object. But there was no room in her case for denials, or puttings off, or any of the customary arts of delay and protracted courtship. Romeo had heard from her own tongue, when she did not dream that he was near her, a confession of her love. So with an honest frankness, which the novelty of her situation excused, she confirmed the truth of what he had before heard, and addressing him by the name of *fair Montague* (love can sweeten a sour name), she begged him not to impute her easy yielding to levity or an unworthy mind, but that he must lay the fault of it (if it were a fault) upon the accident of the night which had so strangely discovered her thoughts. And she added, that though her behavior to him might not be sufficiently prudent, measured by the custom of her sex, yet that she would prove more true than many whose prudence was dissembling, and their modesty artificial cunning.

Romeo was beginning to call the heavens to witness, that nothing was farther from his thoughts than to impute a shadow of dishonor to such an honored lady, when she stopped him, begging him not to swear; for although she joyed in him, yet she had no joy of that night's contract: it was too rash, too unadvised, too sudden. But he being urgent with her to exchange a vow of love with him that night, she said that she already had given him hers before he requested it; meaning, when he overheard her confession; but she would retract what she then bestowed, for the pleasure of giving it again, for her bounty was as infinite as the sea, and her love as deep. From this loving conference she was called away by her nurse, who slept with her, and thought it time for her to be in bed, for it was near to daybreak; but hastily returning, she said three or four words more to Romeo, the purport of which was, that if his love was indeed honorable, and his purpose marriage, she would send a messenger to him tomorrow, to appoint a time for their marriage, when she would lay all her fortunes at his feet, and follow him as her lord through the world. While they were settling this point, Juliet was repeatedly called for by her nurse, and went in and returned, and went and returned again, for she seemed as jealous of Romeo going from her, as a young girl of her bird, which she will let hop a little from her hand, and pluck it back with a silken thread; and Romeo was as loath to part as she; for the sweetest music to lovers is the sound of each other's tongues at night. But at last they parted, wishing mutually sweet sleep and rest for that night.

The day was breaking when they parted, and Romeo, who was too full of thoughts of his mistress and that blessed meeting to allow him to sleep, instead of going home, bent his course to a monastery hard by, to find friar Lawrence. The good friar was already up at his devotions, but seeing young Romeo abroad so early, he conjectured rightly that he had not been abed that night, but that some distemper of youthful affection had kept him waking. He was right in imputing the cause of Romeo's wakefulness to love, but he made a wrong guess at the object, for he thought that his love for Rosaline had kept him waking. But when Romeo revealed his new passion for Juliet, and requested the assistance of the friar to marry them that day, the holy man lifted up his eyes and hands in a sort of wonder at the sudden change in Romeo's affections, for he had been privy to all Romeo's love for Rosaline, and his many complaints of her disdain: and he said, that young men's love lay not truly in their hearts, but in their eyes. But Romeo replying, that he himself had often chidden him for doting on Rosaline, who could not love him again, whereas Juliet both loved and was beloved by him, the friar assented in some measure to his reasons; and thinking that a matrimonial alliance between young Juliet and Romeo might happily be the means of making up the long breach between the Capulets and the Montagues; which no one more lamented than this good friar, who was a friend to both the families and had often interposed his mediation to make up the quarrel without effect; partly moved by policy, and partly by his fondness for young Romeo, to whom he could deny nothing, the old man consented to join their hands in marriage.

Now was Romeo blessed indeed, and Juliet, who knew his intent from a messenger which she had dispatched according to promise, did not fail to be early at the cell of friar Lawrence, where their hands were joined in holy marriage; the good friar praying the heavens to smile upon that act, and in the union of this young Montague and young Capulet to bury the old strife and long dissensions of their families.

The ceremony being over, Juliet hastened home, where she stayed impatient for the coming of night, at which time Romeo promised to come and meet her in the orchard, where they had met the night before; and the time between seemed as tedious to her, as the night before some great festival seems to an impatient child, that has got new finery which it may not put on till the morning.

That same day, about noon, Romeo's friends, Benvolio and Mercutio, walking through the streets of Verona, were met by a party of the Capulets with the impetuous Tybalt at their head. This was the same angry Tybalt who would have fought with Romeo at old lord Capulet's feast. He, seeing Mercutio, accused him bluntly of associating with Romeo, a Montague. Mercutio, who had as much fire and youthful blood in him as Tybalt, replied to this accusation with some sharpness; and in spite of all Benvolio could say to moderate their wrath, a quarrel was beginning, when Romeo himself passing that way, the fierce Tybalt turned from Mercutio to Romeo, and gave him the disgraceful appellation of villain. Romeo wished to avoid a quarrel with Tybalt above all men, because he was the kinsman of Juliet, and much beloved by her; besides, this young Montague had never thoroughly entered into the family quarrel, being by nature wise and gentle, and the name of a Capulet, which was his dear lady's name, was now rather a charm to allay resentment, than a watchword to excite fury. So he tried to reason with Tybalt, whom he saluted mildly by the name of *good Capulet*, as if he, though a Montague, had some secret pleasure in uttering that name: but Tybalt, who hated all Montagues as he hated hell, would hear no reason, but drew his weapon; and Mercutio, who knew not of Romeo's secret motive for desiring peace with Tybalt, but looked upon his present forbearance as a sort of calm dishonorable submission, with many disdainful words provoked Tybalt to the prosecution of his first quarrel with him; and Tybalt and Mercutio fought, till Mercutio fell, receiving his death's wound while Romeo and Benvolio were vainly endeavoring to part the combatants. Mercutio being dead, Romeo kept his temper no longer, but returned the scornful appellation of villain which Tybalt had given him; and they fought till Tybalt was slain by Romeo. This deadly broil failing out in the midst of Verona at noonday, the news of it quickly brought a crowd of citizens to the spot, and among them the old lords Capulet and Montague, with their wives; and soon after arrived the prince himself, who being related to Mercutio, whom Tybalt had slain, and having had the peace of his government often disturbed by these brawls of Montagues and Capulets, came determined to put the law in strictest force against those who should be found to be offenders. Benvolio, who had been eye-witness to the fray, was commanded by the prince to relate the origin of it; which he did, keeping as near the truth as he could without injury to Romeo, softening and excusing the part which his friends took in it. Lady Capulet, whose extreme grief for the loss of her kinsman Tybalt made her keep no bounds in her revenge, exhorted the prince to do strict justice upon his murderer, and to pay no attention to Benvolio's representation, who, being Romeo's friend and a Montague, spoke partially. Thus she pleaded against her new son-in-law, but she knew not yet that he was her son-in-law and Juliet's husband. On the other hand was to be seen Lady Montague pleading for her child's life, and arguing with some justice that Romeo had done nothing worthy of punishment in taking the life of Tybalt, which was already forfeited to the law by his having slain Mercutio. The prince, unmoved by the passionate exclamations of these women, on a careful examination of the facts, pronounced his sentence, and by that sentence Romeo was banished from Verona.

Heavy news to young Juliet, who had been but a few hours a bride, and now by this decree seemed everlastingly divorced! When the tidings reached *her,* *she* at first gave way to rage against Romeo, who had slain her dear cousin: she called him a beautiful tyrant, a fiend angelical, a ravenous dove, a lamb with a wolf's nature, a serpent-heart hid with a flowering face, and other like contradictory names, which denoted the struggles in her mind between her love and her resentment: but in the end love got the mastery, and the tears which she shed for grief that Romeo had slain her cousin, turned to drops of joy that her husband lived whom Tybalt would have slain. Then came fresh tears, and they were altogether of grief for Romeo's banishment. That word was more terrible to her than the death of many Tybalts.

Romeo, after the fray, had taken refuge in friar Lawrence's cell, where he was first made acquainted with the prince's sentence, which seemed to him far more terrible than death. To him it appeared there was no world out of Verona's walls, no living out of the sight of Juliet. Heaven was there where Juliet lived, and all beyond was purgatory, torture, hell. The good friar would have applied the consolation of philosophy to his griefs: but this frantic young man would hear of none, but like a madman he tore his hair, and threw himself all along upon the ground, as he said, to take the measure of his grave. From this unseemly state he was roused by a message from his dear lady, which a little revived him; and then the friar took the advantage to expostulate with him on the unmanly weakness which he had shown. He had slain Tybalt, but would he also slay himself, slay his dear lady, who lived but in his life? The noble form of man, he said, was but a shape of wax, when it wanted the courage which should keep it firm. The law had been lenient to him, that instead of death, which he had incurred, had pronounced by the prince's mouth only banishment. He had slain Tybalt, but Tybalt would have slain him: there was a sort of happiness in that. Juliet was alive, and (beyond all hope) had become his dear wife; therein he was most happy. All these blessings, as the friar made them out to be, did Romeo put from him like a sullen misbehaved wench. And the friar bade him beware, for such as despaired, (he said) died miserable. Then when Romeo was a little calmed, he counseled him that he should go that night and secretly take his leave of Juliet, and thence proceed straightaway to Mantua, at which place he should sojourn, till the friar found fit occasion to publish his marriage, which might be a joyful means of reconciling their families; and then he did not doubt but the prince would be moved to pardon him, and he would return with twenty times more joy than he went forth with grief. Romeo was convinced by these wise counsels of the friar, and took his leave to go and seek his lady, proposing to stay with her that night, and by daybreak pursue his journey alone to Mantua; to which place the good friar promised to send him letters from time to time, acquainting him with the state of affairs at home.

That night Romeo passed with his dear wife, gaining secret admission to her chamber, from the orchard in which he had heard her confession of love the night before. That had been a night of unmixed joy and rapture; but the pleasures of this night, and the delight which these lovers took in each other's society, were sadly allayed with the prospect of parting, and the fatal adventures of the past day. The unwelcome daybreak seemed to come too soon, and when Juliet heard the morning song of the lark, she would have persuaded herself that it was the nightingale, which sings by night; but it was too truly the lark which sang, and a discordant and unpleasing note it seemed to her; and the streaks of day in the east too certainly pointed out that it was time for these lovers to part. Romeo took his leave of his dear wife with a heavy heart, promising to write to her from Mantua every hour in the day; and when he had descended from her chamber window, as he stood below her on the ground, in that sad foreboding state of mind in which she was, he appeared to her eyes as one dead in the bottom of a tomb. Romeo's mind misgave him in like manner: but now he was forced hastily to depart, for it was death for him to be found within the walls of Verona after daybreak.

This was but the beginning of the tragedy of this pair of star-crossed lovers. Romeo had not been

gone many days, before the old lord Capulet proposed a match for Juliet. The husband he had chosen
for her, not dreaming that she was married already,
was count Paris, a gallant, young, and noble gentleman, no unworthy suitor to the young Juliet, if she
had never seen Romeo.

The terrified Juliet was in a sad perplexity at her
father's offer. She pleaded her youth unsuitable to
marriage, the recent death of Tybalt, which had left
her spirits too weak to meet a husband with any face
of joy, and how indecorous it would show for the
family of the Capulets to be celebrating a nuptial
feast, when his funeral solemnities were hardly over:
she pleaded every reason against the match, but the
true one, namely, that she was married already. But
lord Capulet was deaf to all her excuses, and in a
peremptory manner ordered her to get ready, for by
the following Thursday she should be married to
Paris: and having found her a husband, rich, young,
and noble, such as the proudest maid in Verona
might joyfully accept, he could not bear that out of
an affected coyness, as he construed her denial, she
should oppose obstacles to her own good fortune.

In this extremity Juliet applied to the friendly
friar, always her counselor in distress, and he asking
her if she had resolution to undertake a desperate
remedy, and she answering that she would go into
the grave alive rather than marry Paris, her own dear

husband living; he directed her to go home, and appear merry, and give her consent to marry Paris, according to her father's desire, and on the next night, which was the night before the marriage, to drink off the contents of a vial which he then gave her, the effect of which would be that for two-and-forty hours after drinking it she should appear cold and lifeless; and when the bridegroom came to fetch her in the morning, he would find her to appearance dead; that then she would be borne, as the manner in that country was, uncovered on a bier, to be buried in the family vault; that if she could put off womanish fear, and consent to this terrible trial, in forty-two hours after swallowing the liquid (such was its certain operation) she would be sure to awake, as from a dream; and before she should awake, he would let her husband know their drift, and he should come in the night, and bear her thence to Mantua. Love, and the dread of marrying Paris, gave young Juliet strength to undertake this horrible adventure; and she took the vial of the friar, promising to observe his directions.

Going from the monastery, she met the young count Paris, and modestly dissembling, promised to become his bride. This was joyful news to the lord Capulet and his wife. It seemed to put youth into the old man; and Juliet, who had displeased him exceedingly, by her refusal of the count, was his darling again, now she promised to be obedient. All things in the house were in a bustle against the approaching nuptials. No cost was spared to prepare such festival rejoicings as Verona had never before witnessed.

On the Wednesday night Juliet drank off the potion. She had many misgivings lest the friar, to avoid the blame which might be imputed to him for marrying her to Romeo, had given her poison; but then he was always known for a holy man: then lest she should awake before the time that Romeo was to come for her; whether the terror of the place, a vault of dead Capulets' bones, and where Tybalt, all bloody, lay festering in his shroud, would not be enough to drive her distracted: again she thought of all the stories she had heard of spirits haunting the places where their bodies were bestowed. But then her love for Romeo, and her aversion for Paris returned, and she desperately swallowed the draught, and became insensible.

When young Paris came early in the morning with music to awaken his bride, instead of a living Juliet, her chamber presented the dreary spectacle of a lifeless corpse. What death to his hopes! What confusion then reigned through the whole house! Poor Paris lamenting his bride, whom most detestable death had beguiled him of, had divorced from him even before their hands were joined. But still more piteous it was to hear the mournings of the old lord and lady Capulet, who having but this one, one poor living child to rejoice and solace in, cruel death had snatched her from their sight, just as these careful parents were on the point of seeing her advanced (as they thought) by a promising and advantageous match. Now all things that were ordained for the festival were turned from their properties to do the office of a black funeral. The wedding cheer served for a sad burial feast, the bridal hymns were changed for sullen dirges, the sprightly instruments to melancholy bells, and the flowers that should have been strewed in the bride's path, now served but to strew her corpse. Now, instead of a priest to marry her, a priest was needed to bury her; and she was borne to church indeed, not to augment the cheerful hopes of the living, but to swell the dreary numbers of the dead.

Bad news, which always travels faster than good, now brought the dismal story of his Juliet's death to Romeo, at Mantua, before the messenger could arrive, who was sent from friar Lawrence to apprise him that these were mock funerals only, and but the shadow and representation of death, and that his dear lady lay in the tomb but for a short while, expecting when Romeo would come to release her from that dreary mansion. Just before, Romeo had been unusually joyful and lighthearted. He had dreamed in the night that he was dead (a strange dream, that gave a dead man leave to think), and that his lady came and found him dead, and breathed such life with kisses in his lips, that he revived, and was an emperor! And now that a messenger came from Verona, he thought surely it was to confirm some good news which his dreams had presaged. But when the contrary to this flattering vision appeared, and that it was his lady who was dead in truth, whom he could not revive by any kisses, he ordered horses to be got ready, for he determined that night to visit Verona, and to see his lady in her tomb. And as mischief is swift to enter into the thoughts of desperate men, he called to mind a poor apothecary, whose shop in Mantua he had lately passed, and from the beggarly appearance of the man, who seemed famished, and the wretched show in his show of empty boxes ranged on dirty shelves, and other tokens of extreme wretchedness, he had said at the time (perhaps having some misgivings that his own disastrous life might haply meet with a conclusion so desperate), "If a man were to need poison, which by the law of Mantua it is death to sell, here lives a poor wretch who would sell it him." These words of his now came into his mind, and he sought out the apothecary, who after some pretended scruples, Romeo offering him gold, which his poverty could not resist, sold him a poison, which, if he swallowed, he told him, if he had the strength of twenty men, would quickly dispatch him.

With this poison he set out for Verona, to have a sight of his dear lady in her tomb, meaning, when he had satisfied his sight, to swallow the poison, and be buried by her side. He reached Verona at midnight, and found the churchyard, in the midst of which was situated the ancient tomb of the Capulets. He had provided a light, and a spade, and wrenching iron, and was proceeding to break open the monument, when he was interrupted by a voice, which by the name of *vile Montague*, bade him desist from his unlawful business. It was the young count Paris, who had come to the tomb of Juliet at that unseasonable time of night, to strew flowers and to weep over the grave of her that should have been his bride. He knew not what an interest Romeo had in the dead, but knowing him to be a Montague, and (as he supposed) a sworn foe to all the Capulets, he judged that he was come by night to do some villainous shame to the dead bodies; therefore in an angry tone he bade him desist; and as a criminal, condemned by the laws of Verona to die if he were found within the walls of the city, he would have apprehended him. Romeo urged Paris to leave him, and warned him by the fate of Tybalt, who lay buried there, not to provoke his anger, or draw down another sin upon his head, by forcing him to kill him. But the count in scorn refused his warning, and laid hands on him as a felon, which Romeo resisting, they fought, and Paris fell. When Romeo, by the help of a light, came to see who it was that he had slain, that it was Paris, who (he learned in his way from Mantua) should have married Juliet, he took the dead youth by the hand, as one whom misfortune had made a companion, and said that he would bury him in a triumphal grave, meaning in Juliet's grave, which he now opened: and there lay his lady, as one whom death had no power upon to change a feature or complexion, in her matchless beauty; or as if Death were amorous, and the lean abhorred monster kept her there for his delight; for she lay yet fresh and blooming, as she had fallen to sleep when she swallowed that benumbing potion; and near her lay Tybalt in his bloody shroud, whom Romeo seeing, begged pardon of his lifeless corpse, and for Juliet's sake called him *cousin*, and said that he was about to do him a favor by putting his enemy to death. Here Romeo took his last leave of his lady's lips, kissing them; and here he shook the burden of his cross stars from his weary body, swallowing that poison which the apothecary had sold him, whose operation was fatal and real, not like that dissembling potion which Juliet had swallowed, the effect of which was now nearly expiring, and she about to awake to complain that Romeo had not kept his time, or that he had come too soon.

For now the hour was arrived at which the friar had promised that she should awake; and he, having learned that his letters which he had sent to Mantua, by some unlucky detention of the messenger, had never reached Romeo, came himself, provided with the pickaxe and lantern, to deliver the lady from her confinement; but he was surprised to find a light already burning in the Capulets' monument, and to see swords and blood near it, and Romeo and Paris lying breathless by the monument.

Before he could entertain a conjecture, to imagine how these fatal accidents had fallen out, Juliet awoke out of her trance, and seeing the friar near her, she remembered the place where she was, and the occasion of her being there, and asked for Romeo, but the friar, hearing a noise, bade her come out of that place of death, and of unnatural sleep, for a greater power than they could contradict had thwarted their intents; and being frightened by the noise of people coming, he fled: but when Juliet saw the cup closed in her true love's hand, she guessed that poison had been the cause of his end, and she would have swallowed the dregs if any had been left, and she kissed his still warm lips to try if any poison yet did hang upon them; then hearing a nearer noise of people coming, she quickly unsheathed a dagger which she wore, and stabbing herself, died by her true Romeo's side.

The watch by this time had come up to the place. A page belonging to count Paris, who had witnessed the fight between his master and Romeo, had given the alarm, which had spread among the citizens, who went up and down the streets of Verona confusedly exclaiming, A Paris! a Romeo! a Juliet! as the rumor had imperfectly reached them, till the uproar brought lord Montague and lord Capulet out of their beds, with the prince, to inquire into the causes of the disturbance. The friar had been apprehended by some of the watch, coming from the churchyard, trembling, sighing, and weeping, in a suspicious manner. A great multitude being assembled at the Capulets' monument, the friar was demanded by the prince to deliver what he knew of these strange and disastrous accidents.

And there, in the presence of the old lords Montague and Capulet, he faithfully related the story of their children's fatal love, the part he took in promoting their marriage, in the hope in that union to end the long quarrels between their families: how Romeo, there dead, was husband to Juliet; and Juliet, there dead, was Romeo's faithful wife; how before he could find a fit opportunity to divulge their marriage, another match was projected for Juliet, who, to avoid the crime of a second marriage, swallowed the sleeping draught (as he advised), and all thought her dead; how meantime he wrote to Romeo, to come and take her thence when the force of the potion should cease, and by what unfortunate miscarriage of the messenger the letters never reached Romeo; further than this the friar could not follow the story, nor knew more than that coming himself, to deliver Juliet from that place of death, he found the count Paris and Romeo slain. The remainder of the transactions was supplied by the narration of the page who had seen Paris and Romeo fight, and by the servant who came with Romeo from Verona, to whom this faithful lover had given letters to be delivered to his father in the event of his death, which made good the friar's words, confessing his marriage with Juliet, imploring the forgiveness of his parents, acknowledging the buying of the poison of the poor apothecary, and his intent in coming to the monument, to die, and lie with Juliet. All these circumstances agreed together to clear the friar from any hand he could be supposed to have in these complicated slaughters, further than as the unintended consequences of his own well meant, yet too artificial and subtle contrivances.

And the prince, turning to these old lords, Montague and Capulet, rebuked them for their brutal and irrational enmities, and showed them what a scourge Heaven had laid upon such offenses, that it had found means even through the love of their children to punish their unnatural hate. And these old rivals, no longer enemies, agreed to bury their long strife in their children's graves; and lord Capulet requested lord Montague to give him his hand, calling him by the name of brother, as if in acknowledgment of the union of their families, by the marriage of the young Capulet and Montague; and saying that lord Montague's hand (in token of reconcilement) was all he demanded for his daughter's jointure: but lord Montague said he would give him more, for he would raise her a statue of pure gold, that while Verona kept its name, no figure should be so esteemed for its richness and workmanship as that of the true and faithful Juliet. And lord Capulet in return said that he would raise another statue to Romeo. So did these poor old lords, when it was too late, strive to outdo each other in mutual courtesies: while so deadly had been their rage and enmity in past times, that nothing but the fearful overthrow of their children (poor sacrifices to their quarrels and dissensions) could remove the rooted hates and jealousies of the noble families.

The Lady, or the Tiger?

[FRANK R. STOCKTON]

In the very olden time there lived a semi-barbaric king, whose ideas, though somewhat polished and sharpened by the progressiveness of distant Latin neighbors, were still large, florid, and untrammeled, as became the half of him which was barbaric. He was a man of exuberant fancy, and, withal, of an authority so irresistible that, at his will, he turned his varied fancies into facts. He was greatly given to self-communing, and, when he and himself agreed upon anything, the thing was done. When every member of his domestic and political systems moved smoothly in its appointed course, his nature was bland and genial; but, whenever there was a little hitch, and some of his orbs got out of their orbits, he was blander and more genial still, for nothing pleased him so much as to make the crooked straight and crush down uneven places.

Among the borrowed notions by which his barbarism had become semified was that of the public arena, in which, by exhibitions of manly and beastly valor, the minds of his subjects were refined and cultured.

But even here the exuberant and barbaric fancy asserted itself. The arena of the king was built, not to give the people an opportunity of hearing the rhapsodies of dying gladiators, nor to enable them to view the inevitable conclusion of a conflict between religious opinions and hungry jaws, but for purposes far better adapted to widen and develop the mental energies of the people. This vast amphitheater, with its encircling galleries, its mysterious vaults, and its unseen passages, was an agent of poetic justice, in which crime was punished, or virtue rewarded, by the decrees of an impartial and incorruptible chance.

When a subject was accused of a crime of sufficient importance to interest the king, public notice was given that on an appointed day the fate of the accused person would be decided in the king's arena, a structure which well deserved its name, for, although its form and plan were borrowed from afar, its purpose emanated solely from the brain of this man, who, every barleycorn a king, knew no tradition to which he owed more allegiance than pleased his fancy, and who ingrafted on every adopted form of human thought and action the rich growth of his barbaric idealism.

When all the people had assembled in the galleries, and the king, surrounded by his court, sat high up on his throne of royal state on one side of the arena, he gave a signal, a door beneath him opened, and the accused subject stepped out into the amphitheater. Directly opposite him, on the other side of the enclosed space, were two doors, exactly alike and side by side. It was the duty and the privilege of the person on trial to walk directly to these doors and open one of them. He could open either door he pleased; he was subject to no guidance or influence but that of the aforementioned impartial and incorruptible chance. If he opened the one, there came out of it a hungry tiger, the fiercest and most cruel that could be procured, which immediately sprang upon him and tore him to pieces as a punishment for his guilt. The moment that the case of the criminal was thus decided, doleful iron bells were clanged, great wails went up from the hired mourners posted on the outer rim of the arena, and the vast audience, with bowed heads and downcast hearts, wended slowly their homeward way, mourning greatly that one so young and fair, or so old and respected, should have merited so dire a fate.

But, if the accused person opened the other door, there came forth from it a lady, the most suitable to his years and station that his majesty could select among his fair subjects, and to this lady he was immediately married, as a reward of his innocence. It mattered not that he might already possess a wife and family, or that his affections might be engaged upon an object of his own selection; the king allowed no such subordinate arrangements to interfere with his great scheme of retribution and reward. The exercises, as in the other instance, took place immediately, and in the arena. Another door opened beneath the king, and a priest, followed by a band of choristers, and dancing maidens blowing joyous airs on golden horns and treading an epithalamic measure, advanced to where the pair stood, side by side, and the wedding was promptly and cheerily solemnized. Then the gay brass bells rang forth their merry peals, the people shouted glad hurrahs, and the innocent man, preceded by children strewing flowers on his path, led his bride to his home.

This was the king's semi-barbaric method of administering justice. Its perfect fairness is obvious. The criminal could not know out of which door would come the lady; he opened either he pleased, without having the slightest idea whether, in the next instant, he was to be devoured or married. On some occasions the tiger came out of one door, and on some out of the other. The decisions of this tribunal were not only fair, they were positively determinate: the accused person was instantly punished if he found himself guilty, and, if innocent, he was rewarded on the spot, whether he liked it or not. There was no escape from the judgments of the king's arena.

The institution was a very popular one. When the people gathered together on one of the great trial days, they never knew whether they were to witness a bloody slaughter or a hilarious wedding. This element of uncertainty lent an interest to the occasion which it could not otherwise have attained. Thus, the masses were entertained and pleased, and the thinking part of the community could bring no charge of unfairness against this plan, for did not the accused person have the whole matter in his own hands?

This semi-barbaric king had a daughter as blooming as his most florid fancies, and with a soul as fervent and imperious as his own. As is usual in such cases, she was the apple of his eye, and was loved by him above all humanity. Among his courtiers was a young man of that fineness of blood and lowness of station common to the conventional heroes of romance who love royal maidens. This royal maiden was well satisfied with her lover, for he was handsome and brave to a degree unsurpassed in all this kingdom, and she loved him with an ardor that had enough of barbarism in it to make it exceedingly warm and strong. This love affair moved on happily for many months, until one day the king happened to discover its existence. He did not hesitate nor waver in regard to his duty in the premises. The youth was immediately cast into prison, and a day was appointed for his trial in the king's arena. This, of course, was an especially important occasion, and his majesty, as well as all the people, was greatly interested in the workings and development of this trial. Never before had such a case occurred; never before had a subject dared to love the daughter of the king. In after years such things became commonplace enough, but then they were in no slight degree novel and startling.

The tiger-cages of the kingdom were searched for the most savage and relentless beasts, from which the fiercest monster might be selected for the arena; and the ranks of maiden youth and beauty throughout the land were carefully surveyed by competent judges in order that the young man might have a fitting bride in case fate did not determine for him a different destiny. Of course, everybody knew that the deed with which the accused was charged had been done. He had loved the princess, and neither he, she, nor any one else, thought of denying the fact; but the king would not think of allowing any fact of this kind to interfere with the workings of the tribunal, in which he took such great delight and satisfaction. No matter how the affair turned out, the youth would be disposed of, and the king would take an aesthetic pleasure in watching the course of events, which would determine whether or not the young man had done wrong in allowing himself to love the princess.

The appointed day arrived. From far and near the people gathered, and thronged the great galleries of the arena, and crowds, unable to gain admittance, massed themselves against its outside walls. The king and his court were in their places, opposite the twin doors, those fateful portals, so terrible in their similarity.

All was ready. The signal was given. A door beneath the royal party opened, and the lover of the princess walked into the arena. Tall, beautiful, fair, his appearance was greeted with a low hum of admiration and anxiety. Half the audience had not known so grand a youth had lived among them. No wonder the princess loved him! What a terrible thing for him to be there!

As the youth advanced into the arena he turned, as the custom was, to bow to the king, but he did not think at all of that royal personage. His eyes were fixed upon the princess, who sat to the right of her father. Had it not been for the moiety of barbarism in her nature it is probable that the lady would not have been there, but her intense and fervid soul would not allow her to be absent on an occasion in which she was so terribly interested. From the moment that the decree had gone forth that her lover should decide his fate in the king's arena, she had thought of nothing, night or day, but this great event and the various subjects connected with it. Possessed of more power, influence, and force of character than anyone who had ever before been interested in such a case, she had done what no other person had done—she had possessed herself of the secret of the doors. She knew in which of the two rooms, that lay behind those doors, stood the cage of the tiger, with its open front, and in which waited the lady. Through these thick doors, heavily curtained with skins on the inside, it was impossible that any noise or suggestion should come from within to the person who should approach to raise the latch of one of them. But gold, and the power of a woman's will, had brought the secret to the princess.

And not only did she know in which room stood the lady ready to emerge, all blushing and radiant, should her door be opened, but she knew who the lady was. It was one of the fairest and loveliest of the damsels of the court who had been selected as the reward of the accused youth, should he be proved innocent of the crime of aspiring to one so far above him; and the princess hated her. Often had she seen, or imagined that she had seen, this fair creature throwing glances of admiration upon the person of her lover, and sometimes she thought these glances were perceived, and even returned. Now and then she had seen them talking together; it was but for a moment or two, but much can be said in a brief space; it may have been on most unimportant topics, but how could she know that? The girl was lovely, but she had dared to raise her eyes to the loved one of the princess; and, with all the intensity of the savage blood transmitted to her through long lines of wholly barbaric ancestors, she hated the woman who blushed and trembled behind that silent door.

When her lover turned and looked at her, and his eye met hers as she sat there, paler and whiter than any one in the vast ocean of anxious faces about her, he saw, by that power of quick perception which is given to those whose souls are one, that she knew behind which door crouched the tiger, and behind which stood the lady. He had expected her to know it. He understood her nature, and his soul was assured that she would never rest until she had made plain to herself this thing, hidden to all other lookers-on, even to the king. The only hope for the youth in which there was any element of certainty was based upon the success of the princess in discovering this mystery; and the moment he looked upon her, he saw she had succeeded, as in his soul he knew she would succeed.

Then it was that his quick and anxious glance asked the question: "Which?" It was as plain to her as if he shouted it from where he stood. There was not an instant to be lost. The question was asked in a flash; it must be answered in another.

Her right arm lay on the cushioned parapet before her. She raised her hand, and made a slight, quick movement toward the right. No one but her lover saw her. Every eye but his was fixed on the man in the arena.

He turned, and with a firm and rapid step he walked across the empty space. Every heart stopped beating, every breath was held, every eye was fixed immovably upon that man. Without the slightest hesitation, he went to the door on the right, and opened it.

Now, the point of the story is this: Did the tiger come out of that door, or did the lady?

The more we reflect upon this question, the harder it is to answer. It involves a study of the human heart which leads us through devious mazes of passion, out of which it is difficult to find our way. Think of it, fair reader, not as if the decision of the question depended upon yourself, but upon that hot-blooded, semi-barbaric princess, her soul at a white heat beneath the combined fires of despair and jealousy. She had lost him, but who should have him?

How often, in her waking hours and in her dreams, had she started in wild horror, and covered her face with her hands as she thought of her lover opening the door on the other side of which waited the cruel fangs of the tiger!

But how much oftener had she seen him at the other door! How in her grievous reveries had she gnashed her teeth, and torn her hair, when she saw his start of rapturous delight as he opened the door of the lady! How her soul had burned in agony when she had seen him rush to meet that woman, with her flushing cheek and sparkling eye of triumph; when she had seen him lead her forth, his whole frame kindled with the joy of recovered life; when she had heard the glad shouts from the multitude, and the wild ringing of the happy bells; when she had seen the priest, with his joyous followers, advance to the couple, and make them man and wife before her very eyes; and when she had seen them walk away together upon their path of flowers, followed by the tremendous shouts of the hilarious multitude, in which her one despairing shriek was lost and drowned!

Would it not be better for him to die at once, and go to wait for her in the blessed regions of semi-barbaric futurity?

And yet, that awful tiger, those shrieks, that blood!

Her decision had been indicated in an instant, but it had been made after days and nights of anguished deliberation. She had known she would be asked, she had decided what she would answer, and, without the slightest hesitation, she had moved her hand to the right.

The question of her decision is one not to be lightly considered, and it is not for me to presume to set myself up as the one person able to answer it. And so I leave it with all of you: Which came out of the opened door—the lady, or the tiger?

Sources

"A Modern Cinderella: or, The Little Old Shoe" by Louisa May Alcott from *The Atlantic Monthly* (October 1860).

"The Other Woman" by Sherwood Anderson from *The Triumph of the Egg: A Book of Impressions from American Life in Tales and Poems* (New York: B. W. Huebsch, 1921).

"A Sweet Day" by Ada Cambridge from *At Midnight and Other Stories* (London: Ward, Lock & Company, 1897).

"About Love" by Anton Chekhov from *The Tales of Chekhov, Volume 5: The Wife and Other Stories* (New York: Macmillan, 1918).

"The Kiss" by Kate Chopin from *The Awakening and Other Stories* (Chicago: New York: H. S. Stone & Company, 1899).

"What She Wore" by Edna Ferber from *Buttered Side Down* (New York: Frederick A. Stokes Company, 1912).

"Romeo and Juliet" by Charles and Mary Lamb from *Tales from Shakespeare* (New York: Thomas Y. Crowell, 1878).

"Love in a Garden" by Henry Clay Lewis from *Odd Leaves from the Life of a Louisiana Swamp Doctor* (Philadelphia: A Hart, 1850).

"Mr. and Mrs. Dove" by Katherine Mansfield from the *Garden Party, and Other Stories* (London: Constable & Company, 1922).

"Some Ways of Love" by Charlotte Mew from *The Pall Mall Magazine* (July 1901).

"Love and Lightning" by John Oakum [Walter P. Phillips] from *Oakum Pickings: A Collection of Stories, Sketches and Paragraphs Contributed from Time to Time to the Telegraphic and General Press* (New York: W. J. Johnston, 1876).

"Mrs. Knollys" by Frederic Jesup Stimson from *Mrs. Knollys and Other Stories* (New York: Charles Scribner's Sons, 1897).

"The Lady, or the Tiger?" by Frank R. Stockton from *The Lady, or the Tiger, and Other Stories* (New York: Charles Scribner's Sons, 1884).

"The Love Quarrel" by Agnes Strickland from *The Keepsake* (London: Longman, Rees, Orme, Brown, Green, and Longman, 1835).

"Who Was She?" by Bayard Taylor from *The Atlantic Monthly* (September 1874).

"The Fairy Amoureuse" by Emile Zola from *Stories for Ninon* (New York: G. H. Richmond, 1898)